Birding Across North America

A red-tailed hawk on a statue at Gettysburg National Military Park.

Birding
Across North America

A Naturalist's Observations

Text and Photographs by
Philip E. Keenan

TIMBER PRESS
Portland, Oregon

Published in 2002 by
Timber Press, Inc.
The Haseltine Building
133 S.W. Second Avenue, Suite 450
Portland, Oregon 97204, U.S.A.

Printed in Hong Kong

Library of Congress Cataloging-in-Publication Data
Keenan, Philip E.
    Birding across North America : a naturalist's observations / text and photographs by Philip E. Keenan.
        p. cm.
    Includes bibliographical references (p.).
    ISBN 0-88192-528-4
    1. Bird watching—North America. I. Title.
QL681 .K44 2002
598'.07'2347—dc21

                                                                    2001037623

Two mothers deserve praise and appreciation:
My mother, Mary E. Keenan, encouraged my early interest in the natural world, and my wife, Susan E. Keenan, gave unstinting support during my nearly forty years of traveling, writing, and fieldwork, while nurturing four great children: Philip T., Barbara, Robert, and Gregory. All of these family members have contributed in one way or another to this book and my previous book, *Wild Orchids Across North America*.

Contents

Foreword 9
Preface 11
Acknowledgments 15

Chapter   1 Backyard Birding 17
Chapter   2 The Wonderful World of Warblers 34
Chapter   3 The Golden Swamp Warbler in Alabama 55
Chapter   4 The Legendary Sky Islands of Arizona 62
Chapter   5 In Pursuit of Painted Redstarts and Red-faced Warblers
             in Arizona 72
Chapter   6 Hummingbird Heaven 82
Chapter   7 The Land of the Roadrunner 94
Chapter   8 Brazos Bend State Park, Texas 101
Chapter   9 Florida Folly 109
Chapter 10 Bombay Hook and Prime Hook National Wildlife
             Refuges 122
Chapter 11 Gannets on the Gaspé in Québec 130
Chapter 12 Nesting in Newfoundland 137
Chapter 13 Ducks Unlimited 145
Chapter 14 The White-headed Woodpecker in California 157
Chapter 15 Hurricane Carol 171
Chapter 16 Music Appreciation 178
Chapter 17 An Introduction to Nests 192
Chapter 18 Tools of the Trade 203
Chapter 19 The Evolution of Bird Painting 211
Chapter 20 Favorite Birds, Books, and Photographs 227
Chapter 21 Extinction Is Forever 234

Bibliography 244
Index of Bird Names 251

Foreword

THE ENTHUSIASM Phil Keenan obviously has had in his extraordinary experiences with birds over many decades and thousands of miles of travel throughout the United States and Canada is reflected in his writings. His readers often get caught up in this enthusiasm and feel they are sharing the same interesting and sometimes exciting adventures with the author.

Birding Across North America is not only enjoyable to read; it is very informative. This volume would be worth consulting before going on a trip to one or more of the places whose bird life Keenan describes. Examples are the painted redstart, red-faced warbler, and the many hummingbird species that live in southeastern Arizona; the roadrunner in New Mexico; the swallow-tailed kite in Florida; and the northern gannet, black-legged kittiwake, and various members of the auk family in Québec's Gaspé.

Keenan also describes an exciting encounter with numerous storm-petrels and phalaropes on the New Hampshire coast during Hurricane Carol in August 1954. Caught in the midst of the storm himself, Keenan witnessed these birds where they are rarely seen, far from their haunts miles out to sea.

This book is full of information that would be difficult, if not impossible, to find in any other single volume. Much is included on the feeding of birds and on the habits, songs, nests, and habitats of birds the author observed. Keenan also discusses birds that can no longer be seen, such as the ivory-billed woodpecker and passenger pigeon, both now extinct.

Keenan also provides good information on national and state forests, parks, and wildlife refuges; trees, wildflowers, and other plants; as well as field guides, bird artists, binoculars, photography, and much, much more. As is to be expected, the illustrations complement the text very well, most being done by the author, an expert photographer.

TUDOR RICHARDS

Former president and executive director of the
Audubon Society of New Hampshire

Tudor Richards, former president and executive director of the Audubon Society of New Hampshire, on a Dover Conservation Commission field trip at the Audubon Bellamy River Sanctuary. Dover, New Hampshire, 16 November 1973.

Preface

WHY WRITE another bird book? Based on nearly sixty years of birding with eye, pen, and plenty of books, I think I have some things to say that others have not said. I have always kept a journal, an important element in any kind of recollection process. And, as Donald Murray, a writer for the Boston *Globe*, says: "I have the richness of memory that is a gift of age." In this book, then, I attempt to explore certain historical, ecological, and personal aspects of a life with birds, with special admiration and respect for perhaps the most miraculous—certainly the most compelling and unbelievable—drama in all the animal world. Birds live their lives under the most impossible of conditions, many of them weighing but an ounce or two; twice each year they travel thousands of miles, sometimes nonstop across immense stretches of water, to and from their breeding grounds. For this and many other reasons, I find birds to be truly astonishing.

My book obviously has certain similarities to other bird books, like Kaufmann's *Kingbird Highway*, an account of a young birder's transcontinental pursuit of a calendar-year champion lister, and Dunne's *The Feathered Quest*, a more sophisticated dialogue of a husband-wife listing team's pursuit of birds. My story, however, is more closely allied with Roger Tory Peterson's *Birds over America* (1948). My objective is not to list as many birds as possible in a year or a lifetime, but rather to concentrate on their extraordinary beauty, incredible diversity, and unique drama. (There are more than 9000 species of birds in the world and more than 900 in North America, if you include the rarities, visitors, and vagrants, although fewer than 700 of these North American birds are nesting species.) Nor am I interested in competing with the several excellent regional birders' guides published by the American Birding Association. In addition to a few of the so-called hot spots around the country that I do mention at length, many more are less well known but equally well-qualified sites, at least in my opinion.

My first diary entry dates back to 1941, during one of the first major evening grosbeak invasions in the Northeast, when our feeder became the center of attention for birders from all around. More than a hundred of the sunflower-colored seed crushers wiped us clean each day—and nearly wiped us out financially, too. Then twelve years old, I received for Christmas what was then perhaps the best bird book ever published, *Birds of America* (1917), edited by T. Gilbert Pearson. The book went through several printings over three decades, and includes reproductions of some of Louis Agassiz Fuertes's best painting. Both events combined to generate all the enthusiasm I would need to sustain an interest in birding for the next sixty years.

One aspect of the world of birding I miss more than anything else, as I get older, is the de-emphasis by contemporary writers of the importance of birds to the emotional and sentimental life of human beings. In so many circles today, birding is merely a sport to try and list as many birds—on a daily, seasonal, annual, or lifetime basis—or to see as many marginal accidentals and exotics as possible. These are all worthwhile objectives. Missing, however, is the wonderful flair and talent for prose and poetry of nineteenth- and early-twentieth-century writers who "left us the very essence and flavor of the fields and woods," as Liberty Hyde Bailey expressed it back in 1903. Some of the greatest names in American literature, such as John James Audubon, Alexander Wilson, Henry David Thoreau, John Burroughs, Ralph Waldo Emerson, and John Muir, represent this genre, which has fallen from favor due to, as I see it, the fear of being branded too anthropomorphic by the sophisticated scientific community.

This book's publication also reflects the fact that more than 65 million Americans consider themselves at least part-time birders, spending $31 billion annually for everything from seeds, binoculars, and cameras to travel, food, and lodging, while 27 million consider themselves active birders. Another 3 million hunt ducks, geese, and other game birds, spending $1.3 billion annually on licenses, guns, and travel. Over the last twenty or thirty years, ecotourism has become big business as the result of this exploding interest. More people are involved with birds in one way or another than watch all the professional baseball, basketball, football, and golf games combined!

Nevertheless, Americans are generally failing in our responsibility to demand more from our government and corporations in terms of providing better care for our priceless natural resources. Two exceptions, however, were noteworthy in the twentieth century. First, in 1903 Theodore Roosevelt created the first national wildlife refuge on Pelican Island, off the east coast of Florida near Cape Canaveral. It is now part of the Merritt Island National Wildlife Refuge, which is home to more endangered and threatened species than any other refuge in North America. The other bright spot appeared on the scene more than seventy-five years later: In 1980 Jimmy Carter signed into law the largest conservation initiative in human history. The Alaska National Interest Lands Conservation Act protected 104 million acres in the state of Alaska, just in the nick of time.

In this technical age, some approach birding as an excuse to amass an array of expensive equipment or as a competitive sport in which the one with the longest life list wins. All this is for naught, however, if the birder cannot gaze at the simple wing of a fallen blue jay and be moved by its intricate beauty.

The great Teddy Roosevelt once said: "A nation behaves well if the natural resources and assets which one generation turns over to the next are increased and not impaired in value." Unfortunately, Congress and many states have not done very well recently in regard to funding our national and state parks, wildlife refuges, and forests. John Muir put it succinctly: "The battle for conservation will go on endlessly. It is part of the universal warfare between right and wrong."

Finally, I wrote this book because, as Thoreau said so eloquently: "Books are the treasured wealth of the world. They are more intimate with us and more universal than any other work of art. It is the work of art nearest to Life itself. How many a man has dated a new era in his life from the reading of a book!" Like Thoreau, I believe that books will never become obsolete—the world of the Internet notwithstanding.

Acknowledgments

M Y WIFE, Susan, in particular, helped in my perennial battle with the passive writing style. She also reviewed the entire manuscript. My wife and daughter, Barbara, are strong advocates of the writing process in their respective elementary and high school classrooms.

I am a life member and former director (1954–1955) of the Audubon Society of New Hampshire (ASNH), through which many of my most enriching friendships developed in the 1950s and 1960s. I am most happy to recognize and deeply thank the following Audubon friends: Tudor Richards, ASNH president (1953–1968) and executive director (1968–1982), who is still an active volunteer and birder in his eighties; the late Kimball Elkins, dean of New Hampshire birders in the latter half of the twentieth century; and the late Vera Wallace and the late Connie Casas, two extraordinary and enthusiastic Audubon birders. I am especially indebted to Stephen Walker, one of the current young leaders of the New Hampshire Audubon movement, who also has taken the time to review this book. Thanks are also due to Bob Quinn, a bright star in today's New Hampshire ornithological scene; Joseph Welch of Tucson, Arizona, a retired national wildlife refuge manager and my guide in Arizona; the late Alex Sprunt Jr. of the National Audubon Society, who was the foremost authority on Florida and Southeastern birds in the 1940s and 1950s; and the late Alex Walker of Tillamook, Oregon, also an authority on Oregon and Pacific Northwest birds in the 1940s and 1950s. And importantly, I thank the many authors and artists of the vast literature on birds, most of whom deserve a featured position in the front of this book rather than the traditional

15

one in the bibliography. Furthermore, to all those people inadvertently but inevitably missed in one way or another, my humblest thanks and apologies.

The College of Charleston Foundation graciously gave permission to use John Henry Dick's beautiful painting of the red-faced warbler and painted redstart, which originally appeared in *The Warblers of North America.* The Cornell Laboratory of Ornithology and Marge Villa-nova, in particular, obtained some excellent photos of birds described in this book. Dr. Dan Sudia contributed photographs of Southeastern birds; hundreds of Sudia's photographs of birds can be found at the Florida Museum of Natural History web site. Walter Weber's widow, who is still living in Virginia and with whom I had a delightful tele-phone conversation, gave permission to photograph her husband's fine paintings. The University of Arizona Press allowed me to repro-duce George Miksch Sutton's painting of the painted redstart. The Gulf States Paper Corporation and The Warner Collection gave permission to reproduce the hooded mergansers, common eiders, and several other paintings from the excellent book *Wild Birds of America*, which celebrates the work of the fine British painter Basil Ede. Peter J. Yeskie of Hadley, Massachusetts, allowed me to reproduce his prothonotary warbler photograph. The Cornell University Library gave permission to reproduce the Louis Agassiz Fuertes photograph. The John James Audubon Museum in Henderson, Kentucky, provided a fine portrait of their namesake. Cindy Nelson-Nold contributed a wonderful painting of a broad-tailed hummingbird. Texas Tech University Press gave per-mission to use Wyman Meinzer's photograph on the dust jacket of their book *The Roadrunner.* Also, for the use of several covers of favorite old books, for which contact attempts were made unsuccess-fully, I thank the original publishers and authors. I have rephoto-graphed most of these paintings and photographs with permission wherever possible. Most of the photographs in the book, however, are my originals.

Finally, to my executive editor, Neal Maillet: Kudos for suggesting this, the first birding book ever produced by Timber Press. I extend my sincere thanks.

CHAPTER 1

Backyard Birding

L ET'S BEGIN at the back door, so to speak. Most birders-to-be acquire their interest as children observing the comings and goings of birds in the backyard. I was no exception. After many years and thousands of miles of travel, the bird habitat I know and love the best is the land surrounding my New Hampshire home.

I ground fed the birds in winter for many years, but stopped a few years ago, for three reasons: domestic pigeons, mice, and the cursed squirrels. The pigeon, or rock dove, another one of those foreign introductions by well-intentioned pioneers of yesteryear, got the best of me year after year, despite constant harassment on my part. The turning point came one cold, snowy morning that saw me typically running out the back door to scare them away. This time, one pigeon flew to a nearby crabapple tree. I was not about to let the pigeon off so easy. Despite the deep snow and subzero temperature, I ran toward the tree while slapping my cold hands together, but got no reaction from the bird. Then I slapped my hands once more on arriving at the tree, right under the pigeon. It literally keeled over, dropping straight down into the snow. I'd seen the bird take its last breath, the first and only time in my forty years of bird feeding. The question remains: Was the pigeon that hungry or did he (or she) drop dead of a heart attack? I concluded that hunger was unlikely because of other feeders in the neighborhood. Apparently, this kind of eyewitness account is very rare. John Terres (1980) cites only three occasions where humans have witnessed the natural death of a bird.

Then there is the question of the insatiable appetites of the white-footed mice—cuddly creatures who are clean in their own hiding places, the experts say. For the first thirty years in our home, we never had a mouse in the house, despite leaving the bulkhead open day after day in the summer. (The bulkhead is a great place for taking pictures of my roses with the sun acting as a spotlight at the base of the stairs.) Then one winter night it happened: the gnawing and gnashing of teeth in the ceiling. Later, while I was watching the Red Sox on television, uninvited guests began skittering back and forth across the living room floor. "What's going on here?" I asked myself, as if I don't know. I set traps—the environmentally correct way of ridding the house, right? Wrong. For the first year or two I caught as many as a dozen mice, but they kept coming. Because bird feeders and cats do not mix well, it is D-Con to the rescue, and, presto, the mice were gone.

Now, how do we thwart the squirrels? Most of the time we don't, it's as simple as that. Since I started this hobby as a ten-year-old, it's been a fifty-fifty proposition at best. In my experience and the experiences of the average backyard feeder, nothing, and I mean nothing, works all the time with all the squirrels. Baffles, greased poles, weight devices, chicken-wire mesh guards, satellites, you name it. I've tried them all. The best you can expect is squirrel-resistant results, especially with hanging feeders. One of the obvious problems over the years has been having too many squirrels—each litter consists of from one to nine young. Our yard and adjacent neighbors' are bounded by several dozen hickory trees, oaks, and crabapples, all gourmet foods to these ingenious and voracious feeders. Apparently, this spring (2000) they hit the jackpot. As I write, I can see ten new babies, probably litter mates of the recent spring litter, frolicking around a woodpile and, I imagine, anticipating an expected bonanza at our feeding station.

Gray squirrels tend to be homebodies, remaining within a couple acres of territory providing readily available food, particularly hickory and oak nuts, whereas red squirrels prefer deeper, mostly evergreen woods. Red squirrels do come into our yard and the several hemlocks we have planted, however, but only once have I seen them at our feeders. This past winter a handsome redhead spent part of a day at the suet rack while I was at the window photographing, an example of which is included in this chapter. In the wild, gray squirrels outlive red squirrels by almost five to one: ten years to two years approximately, with the females surviving an extra couple of years on average.

A red squirrel on a visit to our suet feeder. Dover, New Hampshire, 10 February 2000.

I see enormous numbers of gray squirrels as roadkill, but this does not seem to significantly affect the abundance of this promiscuous rodent, around my neck of the woods at least.

Perhaps I should try a squirrel-eradication method reported in the *Dick E. Bird News* (an eight-page bimonthly tabloid out of Acme, Michigan, containing serious as well as ludicrous information on birds). The suggestion originally appeared in Bill Adler Jr.'s *Outwitting Squirrels* (1996): "Scare the living daylights out of them. One man put his feeder on top of his car and hid inside. When a cat jumped on the hood he revved the engine, blasted the horn, and hit the brights. That cat has never been back." Although this gave me a good laugh, I don't think it will work with squirrels. This makes me recall a line from Samuel Beckett: "Fail. Fail again. Fail better."

During both good and bad years, a dozen or more squirrels are around my feeders year-round. There is no rest for the weary. A few squirrels are smarter and more persistent than the others. They seldom stay away for more than a few minutes at a time, no matter what I do. On one occasion I even rescued a gray squirrel that had caught its foot in the wire suspension on one of the hanging feeders. Despite the notorious ingenuity of squirrels, I knew this one was not going to extricate itself without help, and I didn't have the heart to watch it die. Needless to say, no appreciation was shown by the squirrel, who tried to bite the hand that rescued it.

Rest assured, however, we are not the only ones on the front lines. Americans have survived several major wars, the cold war, and plagues; we have even landed on the moon. Surely, some day, somehow, this battle will also be won. In this vein of reasoning, I must point out two types of feeding that seem to be working at the moment. A new feeder on the market has ports that close via guillotine, triggered by the weight of a squirrel when it succeeds in mounting the feeder. The other method involves locating the feeder on a post many feet from a house, tree, or shrub—anything the squirrel can jump from—which means, of course, you sacrifice a close-up view of the birds. On this post and below the feeder, you must construct an oversized cone-shaped baffle at least 2 feet long and wide (at the widest point). All of the commercial post and baffle feeders I have seen and used do not do the job. The diameters are too small, and the squirrel simply maneuvers up and over the baffle. A third method has appeared as this book goes to press: the Droll Yankee Flipper, in which the bottom ring perch spins the squirrel off like a merry-go-round! So far it works. Stay tuned.

Where does one begin in backyard birding, other than the obvious winter feeding? Probably with the landscaping, as I did back in the 1960s. These remarks, therefore, concern a residence in southeastern New Hampshire, where I did most of the planting. Many books and nursery–garden center experts tout such things as pines, oaks, and cedars, for example. Besides not producing crops annually, the needled evergreens appeal mainly to winter finch visitors, some of which are very sporadic in their appearance from year to year. Redpolls, siskins, crossbills, and grosbeaks are not dependable annual winter visitors in our yard. Nuthatches, goldfinches, and chickadees, however, are interested in these foods on occasion. Oak trees also are not annual producers. Heavy crops of acorns and hickories are sporadic, but every few years the blue jays, red-headed and red-bellied woodpeckers, wood ducks, and, of course, the squirrels have a field day.

I am more interested in the annual production of fruit and the birds that can be expected in the backyard every late summer and autumn. Based on thirty years of keeping records, the following plants are regularly the most attractive, starting in early September: the silky dogwood (*Cornus amomum*); gray dogwood (*Cornus racemosa*); European mountain ash (*Sorbus alnifolia*); various crabapples (*Malus* spp.), starting with *M. floribunda, M. ×zumi* var. *calocarpa, M. sargentii,* and concluding with *M. theifera* (tea); Washington hawthorn (*Crataegus phaenopyrum*); firethorn (*Pyracantha coccinea* 'Kazan'); buckthorn (*Rhamnus cathartica*); and Amur honeysuckle (*Lonicera maackii* f. *podocarpa*). The buckthorn and Amur honeysuckle are not only some of the last to ripen but they also retain their green leaves later than most shrubs and trees, having essentially no fall color. These two plants are not natives, and both tend to be weedy with no spring or summer appeal; thus, they are not particularly recommended for those reasons.

This feeding sequence starts in late August and continues into November. It is interesting to note that all of the above plants attract from six to twelve different species of birds each year, with the American robin and starling the only two birds who feed on all of them. In

Close-up of a mourning dove in our Washington hawthorn (*Crataegus phaeno-pyrum*) during a heavy snowstorm. Photograph taken from my windowsill using an Osawa 500-mm "cat" lens. Dover, New Hampshire, 12 February 1988.

addition to these two visitors, our backyard plants also feed the cedar waxwing, purple finch, house finch, catbird, white-throated sparrow, mockingbird, rose-breasted grosbeak, Baltimore oriole, red-eyed vireo, scarlet tanager, northern flicker, yellow-shafted flicker, olive-backed thrush, wood thrush, and hermit thrush. Throughout the winter, the tea crabapples take over as center stage. That's when the cedar waxwings visit on a daily basis, for several weeks—in numbers of several dozen to about 200—until our four trees are stripped. One year we had more than 2000 cedar waxwings in these trees all at once. Needless to say, the fruits disappeared in two or three days. On only two or three occasions have the bohemian waxwings joined their cousins in our yard, and they are a special treat.

The crabapple *Malus* 'Bobwhite' is one of the longest-lasting crabapples with small but very ornamental yellow fruit that retains its color until the temperature drops below 20°F, at least in our yard. This variety is the most desirable for that reason alone. 'Bobwhite' is also an annual bloomer, but the white flowers are relatively smaller and less profuse than several other white-flowered varieties. Incidentally, most

A purple finch at our feeder. Dover, New Hampshire, early February 1983.

A young-of-the-season cedar waxwing recovering after hitting our window. Dover, New Hampshire, 1 February 1990.

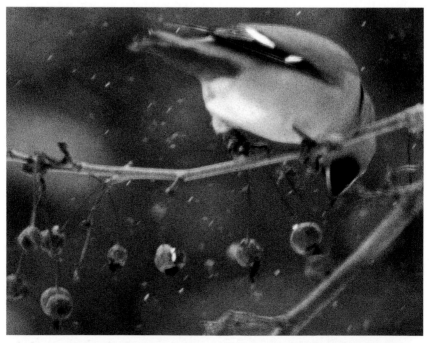

A bohemian waxwing feeding on 'Van Eseltine' crabapple fruit in our backyard during a snowstorm. Dover, New Hampshire, 7 March 1994.

people are not aware that many crabapple varieties are alternate bloomers, which results in good bloom only every other year. In fact, most books list the tea crabapple as an alternate bloomer, but that is not the case with us. I am not sure why, but water and fertilizer might have something to do with it, both of which they get plenty of here. Thus, you should read up on the trees ahead of time or buy from a knowledgeable garden center or nursery. Fortunately, the birds leave the 'Bobwhite' alone until they rely on it as emergency food in late winter and early spring. The colorful fruit of the majority of other crabapple varieties, however, quickly succumb to freezing temperatures, turning brown and rotten early on. We have some forty different varieties on two acres; most of the trees have been growing for forty years or so

A flock of American robins in our *Malus* 'Bobwhite' crabapple, the best late-winter and early-spring bird food for the hardiest northern gardener. Dover, New Hampshire, 17 March 2000.

(crabapples are another hobby of mine). The crabapple is a great fa-vorite of the pine grosbeak whenever it makes an excursion from the north, which has not occurred in our yard for lo these many winters.

One mistake to avoid is planting some of these, in my case crabap-ples, too close to the house, beside a deck, or near a driveway where cars are often parked. The required daily cleaning of deck and cars, not to mention the gutters on the house, is significant and time-con-suming. Despite the great views of the birds feeding in these trees, it makes more sense and far less work to place the trees at some distance from the house. I must admit, though, that I did it the hard way for thirty years, without complaint.

You should be aware that several ornamental landscape plants are so attractive to birds (especially the robin) that they prematurely strip the plants bare in some years before you have the opportunity to enjoy their beauty. Some crabapples fit that scenario, and winterberry (*Ilex verticillata* in several varieties) is sometimes another. Winterberry, a deciduous holly, is my favorite fall and winter ornamental fruit be-cause of its very prolonged (two or three months) and dramatic beauty after the leaves drop. Evergreen hollies, like the Meserve hybrids and

A male pine grosbeak feeding on crabapple fruit on the ground in our back-yard. Dover, New Hampshire, 25 March 1987.

the so-called 'Blue Girl' and 'Blue Boy', are more apt to survive as winter emergency food for birds.

The ubiquitous starling, if allowed to, will eat as much as the squirrels and strip the fruiting trees and shrubs before the native birds barely have a chance. They inundate the tea crabapples at the same hour each day, late in the afternoon in winter, making ours their last stop of the day. (Birds can be very set in their ways.) I can report two good things happening with the starlings that don't with the squirrels. First, persistence usually paid off when I flew out the door and

Winterberry (*Ilex verticillata*) is the best ornamental fruit of all trees and shrubs, bar none, and a native plant to boot. If not eaten by the birds, it persists in good color from October into January and beyond, providing truly outstanding landscape brilliance through early winter. Madbury Reservoir, Madbury, New Hampshire, December 1970.

bombarded them with a rock attack. It required a half dozen or more sorties, every few minutes, but it worked. The birds flew off for good, after a week or more of this routine. Second, in recent years, it seems both the summer and winter starling populations have significantly dropped around here. (Having said this, I was shocked just today over in Exeter, New Hampshire, by the largest single flock of starlings it has been my displeasure to see in years.) Again, I am not sure why, but New Hampshire's short (18-mile) coast with its milder temperatures and less snow, on average, may explain part of the reason for the perceived decrease inland.

I read about successes with controlling gull predation of terns and plovers, cowbird control in connection with the Kirtland's warbler in Michigan, and some others. I see no reason why the same cannot be done with the starling. Several foreign introductions of flora and fauna with few redeeming qualities have proven detrimental to our native populations in one way or another. The house sparrow (or English sparrow) is another bird that seems to have settled down into an urban niche, after originally subsisting on farms and the seeds in horse droppings during the horse-and-buggy days. Somebody feeds them on a daily basis at one of our local supermarkets, apparently year-round. The sparrow population, consequently, has soared to several hundred birds that thrive in a spreading juniper hedge beside the parking lot. The same situation also applies to the rock dove, or common pigeon, which is even more of a nuisance. Again, some people take pleasure in feeding these birds, which they seem to perceive as underdogs. Apparently, these people don't have the foggiest idea about or experience with native birds. I am in favor of managing exotic species, despite some critics, notably the animal welfare community, who seem to have lost a sense of reality.

As mentioned earlier, the starling and the robin are the only two birds in our yard that appear to eat every kind of fruit that grows, especially during emergency situations, such as late winter and early spring snowstorms and colder-than-normal weather. About all that is left by then is the European cranberry bush, a few crabapple varieties with larger fruit than is preferred by the birds in autumn, and the dreaded multiflora rose. Be forewarned when you consider the multiflora: It is easily the most prolific, the most thorny, the most pernicious, and the most hated plant in our yard. It has taken over nearly an acre of our yard as the result of droppings from those birds that have little or nothing else to eat during emergency conditions. A mockingbird lives in one of our large multiflora thickets the entire winter, subsisting mostly on these hips alone. It greets me most every morning on my way out and every evening on my way in. What a price to pay even for a mockingbird. Until the summer of 1999, that is, when "I took the bull by the horns," and bulldozed the thicket out, hopefully for good.

So, where does one draw the line as to who to feed and who not to feed—or whether to feed at all, for that matter? Some argue that, in general, artificial feeding is not good for birds because it makes them too dependent on humans. Others maintain just as strongly that winter feeding is crucial to the survival of several species—at least in an emergency, such as a late winter storm, or in situations where normally southern species, such as the northern cardinal and mockingbird, having expanded their ranges, might not survive without some assistance. In fact, winter feeding stations may be one reason why these southerners have extended their range to the north. Artificial

A black-capped chickadee. Dover, New Hampshire, 13 January 1990.

feeding also has resulted in significant increases in the populations of several local bird species, like the black-capped chickadee. Our plantings are often lifesavers for species such as the robin. A case in point: In January and February 2000 we saw more than 100 robins (a record number for us), probably delayed migrants because of the milder-than-normal December, spend days in our more than fifty crabapple trees. Normal subzero temperatures took over in mid-January and February; without the fruit of the crabapples, most of the robins would probably have perished. Of course, winter feeding stations occasionally provide easy pickings for sharp-shinned hawks and shrikes (the latter are very rare now, however) as well as the neighbor's cats. It is extremely important, however, to follow through on your commitment to feed, every day of the winter. Otherwise, extreme cold, ice, snow, or a few days away from home can result in disaster for the birds. And if you must have a cat, keep it in the house at all times.

This increase in population numbers, however, does not necessarily translate into longer life. Life expectancy and longevity are not the same thing, the former measures the actual years an individual survives, whereas the latter represents the potential life span if not killed by accidents, weather, cats, or hawks—to name a few of the hazards birds face every day of their lives. Also, larger birds tend to live longer than smaller ones. Seventy-five percent of birds die in their first year, but if they survive that first year, things can get better for some of them. One of the only ways to determine this is through banding.

Officially, bird banding began in 1920 and is administered by the Fish and Wildlife Services of both Canada and the United States. More than 50 million birds have been banded in these two countries since 1920. Of that number, far less than 1 percent have been recovered, but that small number reveals some very worthwhile and interesting information. Some of the chickadees I have been feeding, for example, may be as much as six or seven years old, with a few reaching a dozen years. The same is true of our friend the downy woodpecker. The cardinal does a little better, and one in captivity reached the ripe old age of twenty-eight. Robins survive a dozen years or so, if they are lucky, of course, and seventeen years or more in captivity. The all-time records in the wild include bald eagles (twenty-two years), herring gull (twenty-seven), and great blue heron (twenty-three). Others, mostly the larger birds, have lived into their sixties in captivity, and one great horned owl actually became a centenarian. But, again, most birds are killed in their first year from numerous causes, such as predators, man-made migration hazards (skyscrapers, lighthouses, television and radio towers), hurricanes, and floods.

Sharp-shinned and Cooper's hawks occasionally visit us in winter, perhaps as many as a dozen times over the years, usually when it is the coldest and snowiest. These raptors are seeking readily available food. At such times, the chickadees and all other birds disappear as if by magic, remaining eerily silent, until I finally notice the desertion of the feeders and the utter silence. I look out and discover the hawk surveying the feeding station from a comfortable tree perch in a corner of the yard. Once, while working at my desk, a starling was feeding on the suet directly in front of me outside the window, in a sheltered corner of the house. Suddenly, I heard a crash and looked up just in time to see the starling in the clutches of a Cooper's hawk, who, just as quickly as he arrived, did a 90° degree turn and sped off to the nearby trees to feast on its prize. No wonder birds are a bundle of nerves in the daily drama of hunter and hunted.

Terres (1980) reminded us of the importance of a certain amount of predation, by citing the mathematical formula predicting the increase of a species without predators: In ten years, a pair of robins raising two broods of four young each year would produce almost 20 million robins. Notwithstanding this statistic, it must be stated that cats are the biggest cause of bird mortality. This is an easy figure to come by when one understands the tremendous cat population in this country—an estimated 60 million. It does not require much arithmetic to project the number of killings, therefore, and we know no cat settles for a single bird each year. Even some so-called bird lovers with cats merely shrug their shoulders when reminded of the awful toll. These people refuse to bell their cats (surprising recent research indicates belling a cat does not prevent it from killing birds) or leash them while outside, especially in the nesting season, or keep them in the house or within a screened porch—all sensible ideas, but seldom followed by cat owners.

Domestic cat predation on birds is up in the *hundreds of millions* per year, a terrible toll that could be significantly reduced with a national campaign, I believe. Cat predation is not natural. Cats were first domesticated by the early Egyptians and spread around the world by the Romans. They were introduced here in the 1800s to kill the rats that were spreading disease. The bottom line, in my opinion, is the same for so many of our problems: Become an activist. Work with local and state legislators to enact and enforce free-roaming cat controls. Besides, it has been demonstrated that cats live longer with an indoor lifestyle—seventeen years and more according to the Humane Society. Cats allowed free rein outdoors are lucky to reach five years of age. Those people who abandon cats, believing they can take care of themselves because, after all, they are cats and instinctively survive in the wild, are wrong. The survival rate is less than two years.

Two other activities continue to befuddle me in terms of humans' indifference to nature. Why do farmers, for example, continue their practice of mowing hay in early or mid-June rather than waiting until the end of the month or early July? This difference of a week or two could save many bobolink and meadowlark lives, without causing hardships to the farmer. Farmers can only mow twice each summer, regardless of the timing. Apparently, habits and tradition are hard to break. What a pity.

I look back at one of my earliest diary entries, dated 9 November 1941: "Today I saw more birds than I've ever seen, I think: 13 chickadees, 28 goldfinches, 7 blue jays, 4 downy woodpeckers, 1 hairy, 35 meadowlarks, and 1 crow. I saw the meadowlarks at Houl's field." This note from the beginning of my life with birds reveals two things. First, I saw thirty-five meadowlarks and only a single crow. I have never seen as many meadowlarks at one time in the fifty years since, while crows have become abundant everywhere. The second point concerns Houl's field, which is now covered with houses—including my own!

The second human activity applies to every homeowner, not just the farmer. In North America, more than seventy-five species of birds (as well as some mammals) are either partially or entirely dependent on cavities in live and dead trees. Many of these species are songbirds (for example, bluebirds, swallows, nuthatches, chickadees, woodpeckers), but also include hawks (kestrel), most owls, and even ducks (wood, mergansers, goldeneyes, and whistling-ducks in the Southwest). Why do Americans have the short-sighted view that old and dying is bad? Some foresters think old trees need to come down for the health of the forest. Some homeowners are neat freaks when it comes to cutting out dead timber, and some also feel the need to rake up pine needles in their yards. Whatever the reasons, the point to keep in mind is that dead wood is one of the most valuable resources in the entire landscape. Dead and dying trees provide nesting sites for a diversity of wildlife and offer favored lookouts and feeding points for a lot of birds. Besides, eventually, most dead trees are knocked down by storms and wind, anyway, at which time the wood can be salvaged. In the meantime, why not let them carry out their function as nesting sites and lookouts?

In concluding this chapter on backyard birding, I quote from another early diary entry dated 30 December 1941, my third winter of feeding birds: "I've gotten the chickadee to eat out of my hand—and lips, believe it or not. Fun it is. The first time I put a sunflower seed between my lips and a chickadee came, jumped on my coat, then to my collar, took the seed and flew away. Thrilling. They do it a lot now." Many years later I renewed this familiarity with the chickadee in a bit of wilderness I fell in love with and bought in Barrington, New Hampshire. The land had wild orchids, mountain laurel, and pileated woodpeckers. Every weekend for several winters, I would spend hours at my feeding station, replenishing the food and hand feeding "my little chickadees." Pardon the bathos or sentimentality here, but this ritual certainly helped to relieve the built-up stress of the workweek. Unfortunately, now that I am retired, it seems there is either not enough time anymore or it is no longer a priority.

CHAPTER 2

The Wonderful World of Warblers

T O A BIRDER, the question, "What is so rare as a day in June?" should be changed to "What is so rare as a day in May?" simply because of the spring migration, especially that of one family of birds. Speak of May and immediately this birder conjures up the unique excitement of days in the woods looking for warblers—against a tapestry of green unmatched in grandeur even by the bright and garish colors of autumn. In my opinion, no other pursuit matches the pleasures derived from hours of birding during the warbler migration in May.

In his classic *The Warblers of North America* (1907), the first in a line of fine books on the butterflies of the bird world, Frank Chapman summed up the feeling admirably: "The very essence of the season is in their flitting forms and lisping voices; without them May would seem a dreary month and the migration of birds lose half its charm." Unfortunately, most people never see this world of beauty or even know it exists. "The wood warblers are known only to the initiated," Edward Howe Forbush (1929) said, "they pass by in hosts in spring and autumn, but only those who seek them patiently will find them, unless as sometimes happens, a severe cold wave drives them out of the woods and into towns and villages, when we may hear of great numbers of beautiful birds 'never before seen.' He who wishes to make their acquaintance must go to the woods and hills early and often."

Heed that last word. Many times birders search for warblers only to be disappointed, with three or four of the more common warblers the extent of the sightings. This has been especially true in the last ten years or so, with the obvious decrease in numbers of Neotropical migrants. But persistence pays off, not only in numbers but in a greater appreciation of the subtle and then remarkable change that takes place in the landscape during this most beautiful month of the year.

On a perfect May day in 1966, when the bluets, violets, goldthread, and wood anemone were blooming and the birches, pin cherries, and iron woods were in the midst of a misty output of green, persistence paid off for me. In a small open glade surrounded by hemlock and white pine, I leaned against a white pine while looking down a steep slope at a gurgling brook coursing through the opening. There, I was protected from the cool breezes and had the best seat in the house. For the next two hours, at eye-level and downstage but within 50 feet, I watched the performance. At least five bay-breasts, two males among them, alternately appeared and disappeared from view, searching among the leaves as well as doing it the hard way, fly-catching. A gorgeous full-plumaged male blackburnian warbler, apparently gorged with insects, took time out to sun itself on an alder branch 10 feet above the ground, changing position twice, each time resuming the fluffed-out sunning posture. Never in twenty-five years have I been so lucky with a blackburnian. With the dark evergreen background and the sun-flooded perch, it was easy to see why most agree that this fire-throat is the most brilliant of our warblers. The black-and-white, parula, Canada, and magnolia completed the picture. "Only six?" you say. But the day was not bad in terms of brilliant color. Inland in New England, seeing six warbler species is usually the minimum for a good day, whereas twelve to fifteen approaches the red-letter category. Fifteen to twenty is the equivalent of super Sunday.

I live in New Hampshire. It is a safe bet that in May we will have a five- or six-day period of cold drizzle (40°F temperatures) often associated with a cold front that sits over northern New England and the Maritimes while effectively blocking a warm front trying to break through from the south of us. These conditions often produce the best warbler hunting in the second or third week of May. One such week in 1974 (23–29 May) probably represents the second best day of May birding that I ever experienced. On each of these days I saw the following: up to two dozen Canadas, more than a dozen Wilson's, a half dozen yellows, and more than three dozen redstarts—about five to one females to males the first day or two, then mostly adult males and immature males later in the week, all fly-catching in the lee of a spill-way at Madbury Reservoir in New Hampshire, practically in my back-yard. On the third day, the temperature rose a few degrees to 54°F. In addition to the four species that stayed here low in the vegetation the previous two days, eight more warblers joined them but remained in the higher trees (except for the northern waterthrush and common

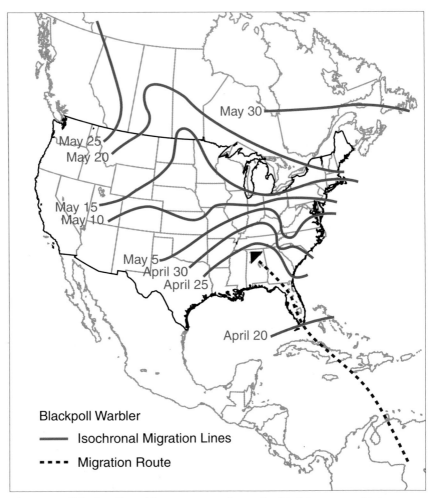

Blackpoll Warbler

—— Isochronal Migration Lines

- - - - Migration Route

This map of blackpoll warbler migration shows the birds' progress during a typical April and May. It is interesting to note that, whereas the birds average 30 miles per day in early May, they move approximately 200 miles per day by late May. This map is based on one compiled by Lincoln and Peterson (1979).

yellow-throat): three immature Cape Mays; two male blackpolls; one female bay-breast; two blackburnian males; and one each of Tennessee, chestnut-sided, yellow-throat, and northern waterthrush. There were more birds to be seen. I watched more than a dozen olive-backed thrushes. Four scarlet tanagers flew about (two females fly-catching and picking off the rocks beside the stream, right at my feet), one of whom was a first of its kind for me, an extremely rare immature male dressed completely in brilliant orange feeding beside the scarlet adult. Even the great Kimball Elkins later told me he saw his first such male only recently. The total continued to mount with a spotted sandpiper beside the stream, red-winged blackbird, field and song sparrows, catbird, phoebe, least flycatcher, black-capped chickadee, and robin, of course, and a constant flying circus of bank, barn, and tree swallows picking off the insects near the water. The highlight of the day occurred when two prime blackburnians came down from the trees to feed on the low shrubbery, even the rocks and bare ground beside the stream

The first scarlet tanager I have ever seen, live or in the literature, with a distinctive red wing bar (or epaulet) on the solid black wing. Parker River National Wildlife Refuge, Newburyport, Massachusetts, 18 May 1999.

—for ten minutes—at one point within 15 feet of my five-year-old son, Robert, and I, who were both sitting on the slope watching the colorful and lively proceedings in stunned amazement. Bob, who went on to earn a Ph.D. in biochemistry, still remembers this early experience, despite never picking up the birding bug. That year was my thirty-fifth in the field with birds and his first, a year that I, too, will never forget.

Perhaps the best day I ever experienced with warblers occurred twenty-three years later, 11 May 1997, on Plum Island at the Parker River Wildlife Refuge, just outside of Newburyport, Massachusetts. Along with Mount Auburn Cemetery in Cambridge, these are two of many classic warbler migration sites on the New England coast, certainly two of the best in eastern Massachusetts. A great contrast between the two spots is viewer comfort. In many instances the birder is almost eye to eye with the birds at the Parker River Wildlife Refuge, which has essentially no high trees, located as it is on a barrier beach island flanked by marshes. The more than 100-year-old Mount Auburn Cemetery, however, provides almost all tall trees in an arboretum setting, which is ideal for acquiring "wobblah neck."

After May's flowers have been transformed into abundant fruit, Parker River's beach plums (*Prunus maritima*) provide important food for many birds in late summer. Parker River National Wildlife Refuge, Newburyport, Massachusetts.

The best days for birding are usually associated with two meteorological phenomena: a warm front coming up from the south with a concomitant tail wind, and a so-called back door cold front backing down from the Maritimes along the Maine coast. Where these fronts meet and stall, the migrants fall out of the skies in huge numbers. Such was the case on this May day. Wayne Petersen of Massachusetts Audubon said, "The numbers of wood warblers observed during the morning hours at the Glades in North Scituate matched anything I've seen at one spot in spring in Massachusetts in a lifetime of birding!" This was true at many locations, including the wildlife refuge and Mount Auburn. In weather like this, the birds come even lower and closer than usual, at and below eye level, fluffing their feathers to stay warm, which makes for an even more spectacular color display. This show was a truly unprecedented experience for a birder, especially one whose favorite family is Parulidae.

The flamboyant redstarts flashed orange and yellow with fanned tails and spread wings, as if performing before an audience, as indeed they were. Redstarts are nonstop hyperactivists of the most dazzling sort, performing fly-catching stunts as no other bird dares, as well as the more routine search-and-destroy method amidst the maze of trunks and twigs. The clownish but splendid little chestnut-sided warbler had a larger and more colorful lemon-yellow cap than most field guides suggest. The magnificent tiger-striped magnolia warbler was out of its element on the grass around the parking lot. The handsome black-throated blue warbler wore his formal tuxedo attire of black and blue and white. I saw the extraordinarily tame black-throated green warbler, under normal conditions only glimpsed and heard (*zee zee zee-zoo-zee*, a favorite song back in the good old days) only in the tallest pines instead of here along the boardwalk. The diminutive male parula, our smallest warbler, a mere 4.5-inch, 0.5-ounce microcosm of blue, gray, green, yellow, maroon, and white, returned again and again to feed among the white blossoms of the beach plum. The yellow warbler, already competing with other males, flew a beeline, making it difficult to discern his subtle maroon stripes. The strictly business black-and-white warbler, in precisely matched zebra stripes, relentlessly moved up, down, and around, like a nuthatch. Finally, skulking on and above the ground was the little masked bandit, better known as the common yellow-throated warbler, one of the easiest of the warblers to pish up. Nature is the artist here, her palette so diverse that human efforts pale in comparison. No other show on Earth can match this display, and all that you need is a good pair of binoculars that focus to 6 feet. One of the gifts of age, Donald Murray says, is the ability to "stop time and live the moment with the richness of memory." Donald Murray, a professor emeritus of writing at the University of New Hampshire, my alma mater, writes a wisdom-filled, must-read weekly column in the Boston *Globe* for those of us over sixty.

Louis J. Halle Jr., in his wonderful book *Spring in Washington* (1947), describes the redstart better than anyone I've ever read: "The male is chiefly black, licked with orange flame on wings, tail, and sides of breast. Few warblers are so easy to find in the woods and to observe. Its behavior and action are its principal charm. It has a way of tumbling down through a tree, from twig to twig, fluttering and falling and darting, as nimble as quicksilver, as sure as a ball in a slot, spreading its black and orange tail like a blazon to the sunlight. . . . If there is a rea-

A male black-throated blue warbler feeding among beach plum (*Prunus maritima*) flowers. Parker River National Wildlife Refuge, Newburyport, Massachusetts, 17 May 1999.

A male black-and-white warbler. Parker River National Wildlife Refuge, Newburyport, Massachusetts, 11 May 1996.

A male redstart. Parker River National Wildlife Refuge, Newburyport, Massachusetts, 20 May 1996.

son for man there is undoubtedly a reason for the redstart. If man was cast in the image of his Maker, I should think that so was the redstart." Without treading dangerously close to anthropomorphism, the more I get into the study of birds, the easier it is to feel that birds do indeed have some form of intelligence and not merely instinct. All a neophyte need do is read Candace Savage's remarkable *Bird Brains* (1995). You will come away with a new appreciation for birds in general and corvids (crows, magpies, nutcrackers, and jays) in particular. More than a century ago, the Reverend Henry Ward Beecher had it right: "If men had wings and bore black feathers, few of them would be clever enough to be crows."

The redstart is dimorphic, which means the male and female differ significantly in color. (Several other warblers do also, the black-throated blue probably being the most drastic example.) Therefore, whenever you see an adult male redstart, it guarantees that he is at least three years old, the time it takes to attain full adult plumage. Most species of birds attain adult plumage in their first or second year. Interestingly, the majority of the sixty or so warblers that live out their lives exclusively in the warmer climes of Central and South America (that is, the non-migratory species) do not change their plumage after breeding. Also the males and females do not differ in plumage, like most of their northern cousins, but are essentially identical in appearance all year long.

Thus, we have both sexual dimorphism, where sexes differ in color year-round, like the redstart and black-throated blue, and seasonal dimorphism, where the male adopts the femalelike plumage after the breeding season. The probable reason for sexual versus seasonal dimorphism involves breeding behavior. The nonmigratory species usually mate for life, whereas the northern migrants do not stay together on their winter range but take new mates each spring upon arrival on their breeding grounds. The males arrive ahead of the females, and bright color is important in attracting a new mate each year. But there are some anomalies, like the waterthrushes, for example. These birds migrate, too, but the males and females look nearly identical. Welcome to the complex world of evolution, which is seldom simple.

Early in my birding career, I prided myself in memorizing Frank Chapman's proposed general laws of color relating to sex and age, which appeared in his classic *The Warblers of North America* (1907).

The laws seemed to help in sorting the confusing spring and fall warblers. It stated: "1. When the adults are alike or nearly alike in plumage, the young in first fall plumage resemble their parents in spring plumage. Examples: *Protonotaria, Helmitheros, Vermivora, Limnothlypis, Seiurus, Dendroica dominica, Oporonis formosus, Icteria, Cardellina,* and *Myioborus.* 2. When the adults in breeding plumage differ, the young of both sexes resemble either the adult female or both adults in the fall." (This second class includes by far the largest number of warblers.) Expressed in another way: (1) When the sexes are alike or nearly alike in color, the fall plumage of both is generally like the spring plumage; and (2) when the male in spring plumage differs from the female, he generally resembles her in fall plumage. There are several exceptions, of course, and Chapman seems to be the only writer who liked his proposal, for I have not seen it espoused anywhere since his time.

The Hellcat Wildlife Observation Area of the Parker River National Wildlife Refuge is a must for birders who want to get close to warblers. In fact, many of the warblers are so close at Hellcat that some photographers are frustrated by the relatively long range of their telephoto lenses and fail to get any images at all. On that May day in 1997, I saw more than fifteen species, in numbers I've never seen before: more than 200 yellow-throated warblers; 100 black-and-whites; 50 black-throated blues; 25 yellows; and a dozen or more chestnut-sided, magnolia, parula, and Wilson's warblers and redstarts. I also watched a mere six or so yellow-rumped, blackpoll, and black-throated green warblers and ovenbirds. Not just warblers, of course; more than fifty species in all, including 20 white-crowned sparrows, 50 blue-headed vireos, 100 ruby-crowned kinglets, to mention a few. I took it all in for five hours nonstop, all along the Hellcat Swamp boardwalk, dike, and parking lot. Many spring migrations, however, are much tamer when the special set of weather conditions are lacking. In such years, the birds pass through in smaller numbers and one must work harder to see them and list even reasonable numbers.

Hellcat in May attracts many of the finest birders in the country and the world. A year later, on 20 May 1998, the Discovery Channel sent a crew there to video a program with Ken Dial of Montana State University as host. It was interesting to tag along with the taping crew, observing the continuous vocal repetitions in getting it just right for the sound and the camera. In commercial television, even nature requires a certain amount of acting. Ken Dial does things with a flair, and I remember an appropriate one-liner characterizing the warbler clan, which he repeated again and again: "Warblers are the pint-sized Olympians of the bird world." I liked this better than another one he threw out: "They are the Pavarotti-Domingo-Carreras of the singers." The former was a reference to not only warblers' long-distance migration flights to Central and South America twice a year, but also to their nonstop movements in general, with the latter statement a bit of a stretch, perhaps, but then again, maybe not.

The human interludes of conversing and comparing birds are part of the fun of birding. There is another benefit: tagging along and listening to others—using their ears—helps me in locating some of the birds I formerly tallied on my own as quick as anyone. As a matter of

A female northern parula warbler feeding among beach plum (*Prunus maritima*) flowers. Parker River National Wildlife Refuge, Newburyport, Massachusetts, 17 May 1999.

fact, I was one of the few who could identify all the warblers by sound alone. But then came basic training in the Korean War and my loss of high-pitched sounds, which includes essentially all the warblers. There is an ongoing disagreement as to the value of pishing up shyer birds like sparrows and warblers. Some swear by it, whereas others scoff at the practice. I think the truth lies somewhere in the middle, like so many differences of opinion. Again, in my experience, most warblers have responded at one time or another to my pishing, which is not to suggest any special prowess on my part. Some professional birders we have known over the years used tape players to draw warblers (or any bird for that matter) into the open for a better view or a better photographic opportunity. I must admit a temptation for that advantage— especially now with my upper hearing range loss—but have never given in to it. That policy, along with my unwillingness to pay $5000 to $15,000 for a super (in more ways than just price) telephoto lens, obviously has cost me on many an occasion in superior pictures. And so, I just complain.

The audience here at the Hellcat Wildlife Observation Area is a relatively balanced one: men and women; schoolchildren to octogenarians; individuals, couples, and small groups. In 1998, I engaged in conversation a very spry, white-haired woman, with the proverbial grin, who drove up regularly from downtown Boston at the age of—get this now—ninety-two. She obviously was proud of her age and did not hesitate to tell me. She and others, I have found, often emphasize two things in particular, a positive attitude and staying interested. I cannot think of any place I would prefer to be, under the right conditions, than Hellcat. That qualifier is important because if you don't hit it right, there can be many relatively uneventful excursions.

After nesting, some warblers take off rather quickly for their winter homes, spending just a few months on their breeding grounds, whereas others take their time heading south, often tarrying through September and October. Most eventually leave the United States, with the notable exceptions of the yellow-rumped and pine warblers, most of whom spend winters in our southern states.

The total number of wood warbler species in the world is approximately 115. Wood warblers live exclusively in the Western Hemisphere, with almost half of these spending their entire lifetime in Central and South America. The other 50 to 60 species migrate north to the United States and Canada for a few summer months to breed. This figure depends on the authority you follow and whether you include hybrids and only breeders: If you count all of these categories, the total is closer to 60. Most species (35) on breeding grounds are confined to eastern North America (including the almost certainly extinct Bachman's), and another four or so are primarily far west and northwestern. Six warblers are Mexican species that barely visit the United States as breeders—mainly in extreme southwestern Texas, New Mexico, and central and southeastern Arizona, while three species reach southern Texas. One of them, the golden-cheeked warbler, is endemic (as a breeder) to a small area west of the capital city, Austin, and nowhere else in the world. The remainder are vagrants from Mexico that rarely penetrate the Southwest every few years, occasionally providing that once-in-a-lifetime feeling for those lucky enough to be in the right spot at the right time.

Landlocked West Virginia, which has the lowest total of species of birds in all fifty states, nevertheless has the highest number of nesting warblers of any state, twenty-six to be exact. The Dolly Sods Banding Station (the Allegheny Front Migration Observatory) sits 4000 feet up in the Dolly Sods Wilderness of the Monongahela National Forest on the eastern Continental Drive, which separates the Potomac and Ohio River systems. The station has been in continuous operation for thirty-eight fall migration seasons and is run by Ralph Bell, George Hall, and volunteer members of the Brooks Bird Club, one of the oldest clubs in North America. In that span of time, more than 160,000 birds have been banded, 75 percent of them warblers in an average year of 6000 birds. These fall migrants are mostly from eastern Canada and New England on their way to the Caribbean, Central America, and northern South America. Half of the banded warblers are made up of five species: Tennessee, Cape May, black-throated blue, black-throated green, and blackpoll, followed in lesser amounts by blackburnians, bay-breasts, and ovenbirds. (I wonder what happened to our most abundant warbler, the yellow-rump?)

The recovery rate of birds banded at Dolly Sods is extremely low, lower than I would have expected certainly, a mere forty-five birds.

Almost all of them are first- and second-year birds. The station's banding record for one day is an amazing 3200 birds, although 500 is the more usual figure; in recent years, the figure is not even close to that amount, sadly reflecting the alarming decrease of Neotropical songbirds in the past ten or fifteen years especially. Statistical evidence continues to mount across the United States and Canada. Rock Creek Park in Washington, D.C., one of the largest urban parks in North America, has been counting nesting species for nearly fifty years. Their numbers indicate that more than one-third of the long-distance (tropical) migrants have disappeared, while the resident and short-distance migrants still nest in approximately the same numbers as they did fifty years ago. Remember these figures next time the subject comes up on how birds are doing these days. Also, bone up by reading *Living on the Wind* (1999) by Scott Weidensaul, an account of the perilous life of migratory birds across the hemisphere.

One of the great mysteries of bird migration, of course, is how birds

A male black-throated green warbler. Parker River National Wildlife Refuge, Newburyport, Massachusetts, 20 May 1996.

navigate. Imagine migrating thousands of miles to Central and South America each autumn and finding your way back to the same spot each spring. Well, that is exactly what many birds do. At night, when most flights take place, the stars apparently play a part in the process, as well as the setting sun, the coastline, major river highways, and other major bodies of water. A tiny amount of hematite has also been found in the brains of some birds, which aids in using the Earth's magnetic field. Of course, some birds are sedentary or nearly so, and others merely come down off the mountain, so to speak, migrating altitudinally. Some species go where the food is at any given time: Numbers of yellow-rumped warblers often remain along the East Coast as far north as Maine during the autumn, after exceptional crops of a favorite food, the bayberry, which happens every few years.

Two interesting, never-repeated autumn experiences with migrating warblers may be of interest here, as quoted from a letter of mine to another dedicated New Hampshire Audubon birder of the 1940s and 1950s, Vera Wallace of New Hampton (outside of Laconia, New Hampshire). The first one, dated 20 October 1953, involves Great Boars Head in Hampton Beach, in those years a great late fall migrant site:

> Two yellow-breasted chats were here for three days feeding on the ample supply of insects that lingered later than usual because of the warm weather, in a tree with a redstart, beside an open-door garage. A commotion inside the garage attracted my attention. I saw a bird struggling against a window, and on the dirt floor below—poised to grab it as soon as the bird became too exhausted to maintain its height—was a cat. My approach frightened the cat and I directed my energies at securing the bird—another yellow-breasted chat—but it eluded my clutch a couple of times, leaving a primary feather between my fingers, finally struggling to freedom through an opening in the stone foundation of the garage.

Another entry from the same date reads: "I remember very vividly a daily visit by a black-throated blue to our grapevine in late September a few years back that lasted nearly a week. I would watch it late in the afternoon and early in the morning, after and before school, as it made several trips to the grapevine. I never determined absolutely whether it was the grape juice or minute insects that were the attraction, but it must have been the former. A. C. Bent (*Life Histories*) mentions this habit in the fall as characteristic of the Cape May warbler, but fails to mention the black-throated blue as another partaker of the grape's sweet juice." Is this an innate or an acquired taste? I don't know, but it is certainly good taste! In more recent times, another warbler attracted some attention even later in the season, this time a one-day visit of the nondescript, olive green orange-crowned warbler, a hardier-than-average warbler that can turn up at northern winter feeding stations occasionally, as it did in our yard on 11 January 1999. And the stories keep coming.

Although the beauty of the warbler family is the main attraction in the spring season, an entirely different set of parameters takes over in the fall when, unlike most bird families, many warbler species go through a drastic color change. One must then play the part of detective and learn a whole new set of identification marks, which takes time—up to ten years of intensive fieldwork, according to the late Roger Tory Peterson, the patron saint of the field guide authors.

Probably the most abundant and hardiest warbler in the eastern United States is the remarkable yellow-rumped warbler. I frequently ponder the reasons for its consistently larger numbers ("querying the familiar," as Konrad Lorenz said). The answer appears to lie within a combination of factors. Although the number of broods produced by most warbler species is still unknown or assumed to be one, a few are well known. Southern species such as the prothonotary warbler, yellow-throated warbler, and yellow-breasted chat have two broods, probably because of the longer southern season. But yellow-rumped warblers in Canada also can produce two broods due to the longer day length for feeding young, or at least this species is suspected to often have two broods. The yellow-rumped probably has the most diverse feeding habits of any warbler; its diet includes all kinds of insects, from aphids to wood beetles and the typical flies. But it is the species' reliance on wild fruit that stands it in such good stead during the long winter months, allowing the yellow-rumped warbler to be one of the first migrants to come up in the spring and the last to depart in the fall. Such things as wax myrtle (*Myrica cerifera*) and bayberry (*M. pensylvanica*) keep it going, along with poison ivy, red cedar, Virginia creeper

(*Parthenocissus quinquefolia*), and several dogwoods (*Cornus*). For this reason it is able to spend some winters as far north as the Maine coast, providing the fruit crop is a good one. The majority of yellow-rumped warblers, of course, head south like their human counterparts, some going all the way to Mexico and Central America.

I have spent many a day at the Maine Audubon Society's East Point Sanctuary in Biddeford Pool watching a couple dozen of these opportunists subsisting on bayberries during an especially good crop year. The birds alternate this diet with some insects among the seaweed and, of course, catch insects, when winter's grip relaxes enough on a sunny day to stir a few. This is wonderful therapy for me during the long months of January and February. Because of this concentration of food-plant thickets along our coasts from north to south, the back dunes of barrier beaches are some of the best places to observe the yellow-rumped warbler in autumn, as I have done at Parker River National Wildlife Refuge on Plum Island. I enjoy the challenge of determining the ratio between adult males and immatures. The former almost always have larger and brighter yellow patches on the rump, side of the breast, and crown and retain some of the gray-blue feathers on the back, whereas the immatures are always browner and duller than the adults, with less yellow in their patches.

September and October are very good months for other things on the Parker River refuge, of course. Peak foliage paints the landscape with the red of winged sumac—by far the most common of the sumacs here—the orange of sassafras mittens, the yellows of black cherry and greenbrier, the pink of *Viburnum*, the scarlet fruit of winterberries, the blue fruit of Virginia creeper, the blue and green fruit of red cedar, to mention only a few of the highlights from the brilliant quilt of nature that spread out as far as the eye can see on this narrow spit of barrier island.

September 1998 turned up an immature fork-tailed flycatcher (perhaps from Argentina) that hung around with several kingbirds for an entire month. Unfortunately it was another example of me not being prepared with the proper lens, thereby missing another outstanding opportunity for smashing photos. On my most recent visit (19 October 1999), I witnessed the leisurely parade of hundreds of yellow-rumps, more than I've seen since the trip to Brigantine National Wildlife Refuge with Bob Quinn and the Audubon Society of New Hampshire a few years earlier on the New Jersey coast. There the yellow-rumps kept up an unending migration along the sand dunes on a similarly mild and sunny day, in company with monarch butterflies that also were enjoying the advantages of a warm day with light northwesterly breezes. On the Parker River dunes I had the most beautiful view of a brilliantly colored, green-backed, female golden-crowned kinglet—completely out of her element—feverishly gleaning what looked to me like slim pickings among the greenish gray false heather (*Hudsonia tomentosa*) that covers the exposed sand dunes.

Whenever a flock of crows sets up a din, it sometimes reflects trouble for a stray owl, which was the case around Hellcat Swamp. A short-eared owl was the butt of the crow's attack and all three birds gyrated gymnastically just above me in the parking lot, as they avoided each other's attacks. About the size of a broad-winged hawk and with the barred tail of that species, the short-eared owl has a distinctive black wrist patch that borders a buffy or whitish patch above and below the wings. The big chunky head (the no-neck effect) is the badge owls carry in flight. Snowy owls call Parker River Wildlife Refuge their home in many winter seasons and are easily seen from the single road that winds north to south for several miles along a sand dune. And, of course, plenty of ducks, egrets, and shorebirds stop to rest and feed during parts of the spring, summer, and fall seasons. There is something for everyone.

Without even trying, the list of birds grows: hermit thrush, brown creeper, white-throated sparrow, slate-colored junco, cardinal, mockingbird, robin, bluebird, not to mention the 400 black ducks feeding and sleeping in the pannes and ponds and a dozen or more greater yellowlegs resting in the marsh grass, only occasionally uttering a much subdued *tew-tew* whistle. The big surprise of this day was the refuge's first coyote: a family of five pups apparently successful in their first try after crossing from the mainland earlier in the year. The coyote was large, tame, and beautiful, wearing a thick and soft tan and beige coat except for the black tip of the tail. She quietly and playfully tossed a blackish mammal in the air, dug from a hole moments before. This coyote seemed to be rather lethargic to me, though, perhaps already aware of its protected status on the island. Lawrence Kilham once said,

"One of the most difficult things to endure for a crow, a wolf, or a human is to feel alone and separated from one's own kind. A sense of belonging is one of the most universal of all feelings."

With a bit of nostalgia, I enjoy recalling one of the remarkable annual events organized by the Audubon Society of New Hampshire that took place every mid-May in the Kensington area of southeastern New Hampshire. Tudor Richards and the late Kimball Elkins, two of the foremost birders in the state during the second half of the twentieth century (with the late Connie Casas and Tony Federer), were the leaders of this much anticipated all-day event. Each year that day usually produced the greatest number of warblers for me—eighteen to twenty —including the currently very rare golden-winged warbler, its cousin the blue-winged, and an occasional hybrid of the two, usually Brewster's. To this day I have yet to see the Lawrence's hybrid. Otherwise my life list—yes I am one of those—includes all the warblers except for Kirtland's (some day I will get to the jack pines of Michigan) and Swainson's in the East (Bachman's is probably extinct) and a handful in the West and Southwest.

For the best illustrations of this family, in my opinion the American Bird Conservancy's field guide *All the Birds of North America* (1997) is a winner. The habitat backgrounds; the multiple identification characteristics; and realistic, accurate, colorful paintings by Larry McQueen and others are superior to the competition, which gets tougher and tougher as the years go by. The National Geographic Society's *A Field Guide to Birds* (1999) is an improvement over the first two editions. And, finally, Dunn and Garrett's *Warblers* (1997), one of the Peterson Field Guide series, presents by far the most complete information of any field guide on any bird family. My only complaint deals with the format; the layout within the species accounts leaves something to be desired in terms of quick access to the information. Alas, the perfect field guide remains elusive.

In their *Birds of the Connecticut Valley in Massachusetts* (1937), Bagg and Eliot called for the changing of several common names, a suggestion that never won many converts, at least officially, but one I always thought had merit. To wit: Canadian or necklaced, Wilson's or golden black-cap, worm-eating or stripe-poll, orange-crowned or green-yellow, myrtle or yellow-rumped, magnolia or yellow-rumped (curiously, no distinction from the former), Cape May or bay-cheek, blackburnian or fire-throat, parula or blue yellowthroat, yellow-throated or gray yellowthroat, palm or bay-poll, black-throated green or green black-throat, black-throated blue or blue blackthroat, to mention a few of the warblers. Many more appropriate names were left as is, of course, such as blackpoll, bay-breasted, pine, cerulean, and redstart. The eastern Massachusetts birding establishment, led by Ludlow Griscom of Harvard at the time, apparently did not think too highly of Bagg and Eliot's book. And so, the body politic, then and now, as well as tradition affects even the birding world.

It is well known to most people that a combination of factors have resulted in the steady decrease of our wood warblers over the past twenty years. Although most emphasis seems to be placed on habitat destruction—both on the northern breeding grounds and southern wintering grounds—my feeling and experience suggest the following are also important: the rapid increase in the populations of raccoons, crows, blue jays, feral and domestic cats, and other bird nestling predators; urban light towers and skyscrapers (which, under cloudy, foggy, and stormy conditions, take the greatest toll of warblers); and, of course, cowbird parasitism. Where cowbird controls are implemented on the Kirtland's jack pine nesting grounds in Michigan, significant increases result in the success rate of the nesting warbler. Gerrone (1999) defended the cowbird for only doing what comes naturally to her, blaming humans for changing all kinds of habitats across the landscape by raising cattle, in the wake of which the cowbirds naturally followed clear across the country. In other words, "humans changed the world that contained a bird that could not change."

I do not buy that argument. The bottom line has to be a pragmatic one. And as much as I would also like to see humans change, as Gerrone suggests, it is just not going to happen. I support cowbird management, in this case controlling the numbers of cowbirds in the general population, as well as starlings, grackles, and crows. Controls also are being placed on extreme situations with the herring and great black-backed gulls in terms of their piping plover and tern nest predation. Management methods are necessary simply because we humans have skewed the natural world so badly that natural predation no longer takes care of these out-of-control situations. The deer crisis is another example, where animal right activists resist the handwriting on the wall. Henry David Thoreau believed that "every creature is better alive than dead, men, moose and pine trees." But that was 150 years ago, and we live in a very different environment today.

CHAPTER 3

The Golden Swamp Warbler
in Alabama

M Y CORPORAL stops the Jeep at the edge of a gloomy backwater swamp. We begin a sluggish slog, waist-deep in dirty
black and burgundy water, dimly lit under a canopy of tall
and drooping tupelo trees. We warily dimple the tranquil surface, hop-
ing to avoid a startling confrontation with one of the main occupants
of this unique setting, the water moccasin. At the same time, I am contemplating an equally unique golden apparition. On a hot Alabama
morning, the corporal and I are reconnoitering one of the glories of the
Southern landscape, the quintessential swamp, which many people
write off with fear and foreboding. A half dozen ringing sweet, sweet
notes suggest something special is about to happen. I only hear it at
first. Suddenly, the bird appears, straight over the black water, as
though sprung by bow and arrow, the bright golden orange head
glowing against dark shadows as it alights on a dead stub above the
water, then disappears into its hole, but not before taking note of us
with appropriately beady black eyes.

   In the words of Scott Weidensaul, author of the book *Living on the
Wind* (1999), I have seen for the first time in my life the "liquid gold of
the afternoon sun, measured out, drop by precious drop," transmuted
into a golden swamp warbler. Writing more than 100 years earlier,
Frank Bolles (1893) described the pull of these wild places for those
who have the eyes to see and the ears to hear: "There is a peculiar
charm in a spot unknown to the many. Its loneliness endears it to the
mind, and gives its association a rarer flavor."

   I am here, however, because in the spring of 1951 the U.S. Army sent
me to Redstone Arsenal in Huntsville, Alabama, in the heart of the Ten-

nessee River Valley. My superior is a corporal from Texas, an enlistee, as opposed to a draftee from New Hampshire, like me. Our mission is to probe the back roads, ponds, and swamps of the 100-square-mile rocket research center, made famous by the arrival of Wernher von Braun, the German rocket scientist in World War II, and currently under NASA's command. Our job is to collect mosquitoes, both adult and larvae samples, to identify and prepare for shipment to the Center for Disease Control in Atlanta. More accurately, *I* do this; my Texan friend merely goes along for the ride, the fishing, and the snake hunting. We get along very well; it is like a nine-to-five civilian job, his Southern accent adding a certain musical flavor to the moments. I go birding after my work, while he continues to fish—all day.

Snakes are his other interest; I am introduced to several water moccasins, among others. Because of the corporal's fearlessness, I learn how to pick up and handle many harmless snakes we come upon, most of which are resting from the intense midday heat under the recesses of cement bridge abutments, where it is relatively cooler and certainly darker. Perhaps this explains the nightmare I later had one night in the barracks of several snakes hanging from the ceiling above my bed. I woke up, bolted into the latrine, and climbed on top of the sink counter—either in a successful escape or awaiting my fate. "What are you doing up there?" a buddy wonders at this unexpected commotion in the middle of the night. I sheepishly jump off the counter when the "all-clear" is sounded in my awakening mind.

Other Southern amenities induce smiles like first introductions. Cotton fields of high school science books come to life as I handle and marvel at my first cotton bolls (the round seed vessels that split, exposing the soft white cotton). I run across five-lined skinks, notorious for shedding their tails when caught, only to grow new ones; they turn out to be utterly commonplace in the Tennessee Valley. One of the premier southern birds is the well-named cerulean warbler, our bluest warbler, which loves to romp in the tops of the tallest hardwoods. I have a field day around the 100 square miles of open space of the Redstone Arsenal. The equally handsome but more boldly patterned hooded warbler is more accommodating near the ground, as is the demure, leaf-litter-colored worm-eating warbler. The yellow-throated and Kentucky warblers are also new birds for me during this two-year stint in Alabama, all southern specialties.

A cerulean warbler feeding its young. Photograph by Bill Dyer, courtesy of the Cornell Laboratory of Ornithology.

A male hooded warbler. Painting by Walter Weber, courtesy of the estate of Walter Weber.

In his excellent *Florida Bird Life* (1954), Alex Sprunt Jr. said: "It is probably inevitable that some birds will appeal to one more than others. Certainly, this is true, as far as the writer is concerned, for the prothonotary warbler. To him, this beautiful creature has always seemed the very essence of the cypress country. Nothing prosaic fits it." In the same vein of appreciation, a Dr. Eugene Murphy said, "So much is the golden flash of the prothonotary part of the swamp picture that its absence could be likened only to the omission of some important instrument from an orchestra or a primary color from a painter's palette."

I frequently recall the association of the prothonotary warbler with an incident that occurred in Washington, D.C., one that most people have long since forgotten. Three years prior to my induction into the Army, while at the University of New Hampshire, the famous case of Alger Hiss versus Whittaker Chambers occupied the news for several years. Hiss was eventually convicted of perjury in January 1950. In 1948, Chambers originally accused Hiss of being a member of his underground courier group within the Communist Party, while working for the federal government. Richard Nixon, then a representative from California, was on the investigation committee. Chambers was an editor of *Time* magazine before resigning during the investigation. What really caught my attention and interest, however, was reference to the prothonotary. Nixon had asked Chambers if Hiss had any hobbies that he might remember. "Yes," he said, "Hiss was a birdwatcher." "Did he ever mention any special birds?" Chambers replied, "Yes, a prothonotary warbler. He said he had seen one around Glen Echo (near the C&O canal outside Washington)." The next day—with Hiss under questioning—the dialogue went like this, according to *Time*:

> Committee investigator Stripling to Pennsylvania representative John MacDowell: "Why Mac, you're an ornithologist aren't you?"
> MacDowell: "Yes, I am."
> Stripling: "By the way, Mr. Hiss, did you ever see a Prothonotary warbler?"
> Hiss: "Yes I have. It's a beautiful bird. I saw one down at the Chesapeake and Ohio canal."

That did it for me, of course, and marked the prothonotary as a must-see.

The prothonotary flies and feeds low over water with projecting stems and stubs, but sings and hides high in the branches, according to Audubon, who inaccurately stated that the nest is hung at the fork of a twig above the water. The birds do nest in some crazy places at times, however, such as old cans, pails, or milk cartons, but mostly in cavities of dead tree stubs that stand in water, often woodpecker holes. The prothonotary is the only warbler in the eastern United States that nests in natural cavities. (Lucy's, in the Southwest, is the only other.) Bluebird boxes along wooded streams work well also. John Henry Dick's watercolor of the prothonotary in the *Warblers of North America* (Griscom and Sprunt 1957) is a favorite, with the Spanish moss laden swamp background.

Some people have difficulty with the more formal name of prothonotary, but I think George Lowery Jr., author of the excellent *Louisiana Birds* (1955), had the perfect answer for those people:

A male prothonotary warbler. Quabbin Reservoir, Belchertown, Massachusetts. Photograph by Peter J. Yeskie.

Beginners often look with disfavor on this name. Actually, however, the title Prothonotary (pronounced pro-thon'-o-tary) possesses the same high degree of distinction and appropriateness that we recognize in the name of the cardinal. For centuries of ecclesiastical history, the prothonotary, who is legal advisor to the pope, has worn yellow vestments, as the cardinals have worn red. The name golden swamp warbler tells us nothing we do not already know the moment we see the bird; and, while it is perhaps desirable that many names should be of this purely descriptive sort, it is certainly refreshing to find an occasional one that widens our horizons by providing a challenge to our intellectual curiosity.

This species is very abundant in Louisiana and thus familiar to every fisherman of the state's numerous swamp lakes, ponds, and bayous. The status of the prothonotary continues to be stable in most of its range: the river systems of the Mississippi and those of the southeastern coastal plain. Only the usual curse of loss of habitat, both here and in its winter home, which ranges from southern Mexico to northern South America, could eventually pose a threat. On a local scale, however, the brown-headed cowbird is a frequent nest intruder.

Redstone Arsenal is not the only attraction in the Tennessee Valley. Nearby is the famed Wheeler National Wildlife Refuge, the first national wildlife refuge overlaid on a power dam project—the refuge shares part of the resulting reservoir created by the dam. This land was set aside in 1938 as an experiment to see if wildlife could coexist with a power project. The results were so good that the idea spread across the United States and throughout the world. In winter, 15,000 acres of the reservoir's middle third provide food and rest for 30,000 geese (Canada and snow) and 70,000 ducks representing twenty-two species. Here I watched, at length, more new ducks than any other time in my life: mallards and blacks, of course, but also wood, ruddy, gadwall, redhead, widgeon, shoveler, canvasback, and both blue-winged and green-winged teals. Most of these were rare or very uncommon in the Northeast during the 1940s and 1950s. Since then, however, many have become regulars and are even common in such places as Parker River National Wildlife Refuge in Newburyport, Massachusetts.

I have two regrets concerning those Army years in Alabama. First is the loss of my letters back home, which I purposely used as journals to be saved for future reference. But, somehow, they were inadvertently discarded over the years in my mother's home. Second, I never returned to Huntsville and the Redstone Arsenal; things just didn't work out. From a sleepy, segregated town of about 12,000, Huntsville exploded to more than 100,000 people within ten years of my departure, reflecting the power and influence of a military research installation. I might very well have been disappointed, if not shocked, by the inevitable changes that take place under such conditions.

CHAPTER 4

The Legendary Sky Islands of Arizona

O NCE in a while it is good to take the advice of Annie Dillard: "I don't do housework. Life is too short. Let the grass die. If you want to take two years to write a book, you have to take that time, or the time will take you by the hair and pull you toward the grave. There are all kinds of ways to live. You can take your choice. You can keep a tidy house, and when St. Peter asks you what you did with your life, you can say, I kept a tidy house." So, up, up, and away, to Tucson, Arizona, for a month of birding, botanizing, and sightseeing in the sky islands of southeastern Arizona—what a wonderful metaphor for a remarkable corner of the United States.

Geographers and geologists tell us that the southern terminus of the Rocky Mountains is the Sangre de Cristo (Spanish for "blood of Christ") range near Taos and Sante Fe, in northern New Mexico, and the Santa Catalinas northeast of Tucson, in southeastern Arizona. The mountains south of Tucson nearest to the Mexican border, in contrast, are outlier extensions of the Sierra Madre (Spanish for "mother range") in northern Mexico. The most famous of these so-called sky islands are the Huachucas (Apache for "thunder mountain"), the Santa Ritas, and the Chiricahuas (Opata for "big mountain" or Apache for "land of the standing-up rocks," depending on who you read). These mountains rise like massive monadnocks, providing suitable habitat for several Mexican species of birds and mammals in the midst of the surrounding inhospitable desert. These migrant birds are the objects of our attention during the first two weeks of August 1997. (The second annual North American Native Orchid Alliance meeting in Tucson is also part of the modus operandi.)

In addition to the birds, history, geology, archaeology, landscape, and Native American cultures come alive in these mountains. You can spend endless hours doing whatever happens to turn you on in this region; it becomes simply a matter of prioritizing. High on our priority list is Cave Creek Canyon near the hamlet of Portal in the Chiricahuas and Madera Canyon in the Santa Ritas, two world-class birding areas that are always included in the top ten North American hot spots. More species of birds are found in these border ranges than any other comparable land-bounded region in the entire United States. Both canyons are within the Coronado National Forest, a noncontiguous group of units totaling 1.7 million acres and encompassing twelve mountain ranges. Don Francisco Vásquez de Coronado, for whom the forest is named, explored this corner of Arizona in 1540, when it was still part

Cathedral Rocks in the Chiricahua Mountains, showing some of the unusual, colorful, green and orange uplifted laval landscape. Portal, Arizona, August 1997.

of Mexico, searching for the legendary Seven Golden Cities of Cíbola, only to be disappointed.

We get to the Chiricahuas by the recommended route, which is about three hours longer than the short-cut dirt road over the mountain via Onion Saddle and Paradise, Arizona. With a rental car, however, we decide to take Interstate 10 east from Tucson all the way to the New Mexico border—about 145 miles—to the hamlet of Road Forks, where we pick up State Highway 80 south for another 27 miles and then take the right turn for Portal, Arizona, a point on Route 80 about 2 miles north of Rodeo, New Mexico. Then we drive another 8 miles northwest to Portal, the eastern gateway into the Chiricahuas. The massive Chiricahua monolith makes for dramatic company, ahead and just to the right, most of the 27 miles on this lonely, low-traffic highway. Upon arrival at the mighty Chiricahuas late in the afternoon of 4 August 1997, I am struck by the view at the entrance to Cave Creek Canyon, worthy of national monument status in its own right, according to many veteran travelers. Because Arizona has so much spectacular scenery (interspersed with monotonous desert) and is home to several national parks and monuments, the southeastern corner of the state takes a relative back seat. One exception, however, is the Chiricahua National Monument, located on the western side of this monstrous mountain.

At the end of the dirt road in the South Fork picnic area parking lot, a family of six young coatimundi rummage in the vegetation with their mother. The cinnamon brown coatis move quickly, running this way and that while staying close together, their long, ringed tails held almost straight up. They search the ground with pointed snouts and forepaws, looking for insects, lizards, birds' eggs, fruits, and seeds. The coatimundi remind me of raccoons (they are members of the same family), but larger. On average, they are 4.5 feet long—a good part of this is the tail, which is as long as the head and body combined. The mother keeps a constant eye on us, especially if one of her young lags behind the rest, to see where we are at that moment and what we may be up to, which is photographing them, moving carefully closer with zoom lens. The coati defends its young with sharp canine teeth when cornered, but here she is relatively tame, apparently familiar enough to trust the tourist. They are just as capable in the trees, it is said, leaping like monkeys, hissing as they go about their business. This tropical cousin to the raccoon roams all the way through Mexico and Central America into northern South America.

Soon a van full of birders from Canada pulls up to see what the commotion is about. This proves a bit too much for the band of wanderers, who exit the stage almost magically fast. My slides turn out to be less than ideal because of the constant motion of the coatis, but the unexpected pleasure is an exciting beginning. In another part of the woods, the Coues form of the white-tailed deer feeds leisurely while I snap away from the car window. There are no trogons or warblers. Only fifteen minutes earlier we were in the heat of the Chihuahuan Desert, where a desert jackrabbit loped away from the side of the road as we pass by. What a country!

Back around the lodge, a short walk before supper turns up a pair of western kingbirds feeding their young, the favorite bird of Kenn Kaufmann at an early age in Kansas. It also reveals the ubiquitous juxtaposition of house finches and house sparrows; in fact, they are the most abundant bird in town, as in so many other places across the country.

At six o'clock the next morning, under sunny, calm, and quite warm skies, I am up with the birds, specifically, a covey of more than two dozen Gambel's quail, gamboling and *chi-ca-go*-ing in a mad rush across the open road. They are followed by several other birds, most notably a lesser goldfinch, hooded oriole, canyon towhee, and blue grosbeak. Later, we pick up Susan at the motel and drive again into Cave Creek Canyon, stopping first at the home of the Spoffords, a spot famous for hummingbirds, and a highlight for many of the 15,000 annual visitors to their backyard. It is a big disappointment today (confirmed by other people on our morning and afternoon stops) with only a pair of black-chins and little else. Apparently, the day is too hot for everything except lots of house finches and a surprise pair of black phainopeplas, which look like black cardinals with a crest, who alight on the topmost branch of tree, survey the view, and quickly take off for cooler climes. Hummingbirds are the major attraction for many birders in Arizona (see chapter 6), with July and August the best months because they include the newborn and the early migrants. The annual Southwest Wings Birding Festival, held in Sierra Vista, Arizona, one of the prosperous new towns benefiting from the influx of birders from all over the world, usually produces a dozen hummers each year.

A western kingbird. Photograph by J. Woodward, courtesy of the Cornell Laboratory of Ornithology.

Near the junction of Cave Creek Road and the road to the American Museum of Natural History's Southwest Research Station, under the protective shade and cover of the Madrean pine/oak woodland (mostly Arizona sycamore, Gambel's oak, alligator juniper), we stop the car and walk both roads, in search of the painted redstart and elegant trogon, elusive to this point, despite the fact that up to ten pairs have been nesting near the campground in recent years. The nesting season is over now, however, and adults turn silent in August. A couple of other people stop and tell us the trogons are indeed around.

Persistence finally pays off. First a gorgeous male flashes by and disappears up the road as quick as a wink. A few minutes later Susan sees a perched bird just a few feet off the road and gives me a call to come back. Sure enough, the fabled trogon poses for its portrait—a fully grown young of the season, brown with the characteristic white com-

An unusual photograph of a young elegant trogon just before being fed by a female. Cave Creek Canyon, Portal, Arizona, 5 August 1997.

ma behind the eye. I use a 70–300-mm Sigma zoom; the bird even allows a dash back to the car to change to a 400-mm telephoto. On my return to the tripod set up beside the road, the male is joined and fed by the female, similarly colored except for a wash of red on her lower belly. Another picture of the two together caps an altogether intriguing fifteen minutes, and they suddenly fly off together. As we take time to reflect on our first encounter with the rightly named elegant trogon, several acorn woodpeckers and Mexican jays fly back and forth in muted conversational tones, while nearby, another poser, a Hutton's vireo, sits contemplating his world. The bird reminds me of the ruby-crowned kinglet back home: identical color, partial eye-ring, two wing bars, but without the nervous twitching of the wings, and much less active, indeed lethargic is the more accurate word.

After supper, the urge to make full use of the daylight hours at this beguiling spot takes me back up the canyon road for another view of its inhabitants. Dusk is falling rapidly because of the high cliffs that have blocked the sun for some time now, with nary a bird in view or earshot. Am I too late? Not at all. What a difference 50 feet can make: Before you know it, I am surrounded by a dozen or more Mexican jays investigating the intrusion with a ground swell of subdued *wink* calls. I obviously disturbed their roost. This jay is very common at Cave Creek; the birds travel in groups, and, according to recent studies, demonstrate a certain amount of altruistic behavior to members of the family. At the same time, I catch a dim view of a smaller bird flitting actively through the midsection of an oak tree—a warbler for sure. Into focus comes the nattily dressed black-throated gray warbler, not quite ready to settle down for the night. I watch until darkness envelops us both.

The canyon cliffs' hallowed walls are strawberry colored, with lemon green stains. I find myself looking up at every opportunity to marvel at this outstanding scenery. I wonder how the numerous grottos got there, while trying to identify the calls of several owls and admiring the speed of the white-throated swifts flying back and forth in front of the cliff facades. According to geologists, violent eruptions from nearby volcanoes spewing volcanic ash (rhyolite) some 15–20 million years ago created these holes in the wall, or grottos, when the trapped gas escaped by smaller more localized explosions. History tells us that

An acorn woodpecker. Painting from the early 1900s by Louis Agassiz Fuertes.

the last of the Native people in the region, the Chiricahua Apache, apparently used these caverns for burial grounds. But only one has ever been discovered in the Chiricahuas because they were so well concealed. (It is illegal to disturb any of these areas, even if one could climb up to them.)

About sixty species of birds can be seen in downtown Portal, which consists of only a dozen or so buildings. Some of my firsts include Gambel's quail, white-winged dove, acorn woodpecker, western wood-pewee, black phoebe, western kingbird, black-throated gray warbler, black-headed and blue grosbeaks, canyon towhee, hooded oriole, and lesser goldfinch. And, of course, many more can be found up the road in Cave Creek, as I have already mentioned. The northern cardinal appears a tad out of place here to us Easterners, but sure enough, it reaches its southwestern limit in this part of Arizona and adjoining Mexico.

Having grown up in the East, the so-called life zones of C. Hart Merriam (1894) had little practical application for me until I experienced first-hand the wonderful sky islands of the American Southwest. Traveling under the searing sun along what sometimes seem like endless miles of monotonous, flat, straight desert landscape, the thought, "Why am I here in August?" does occasionally surface. But when we arrive at one of the sky island oases near the Mexican border, I immediately understand the phenomenon that Merriam experienced near Flagstaff, Arizona, in the San Francisco Mountains, just a few hours' ride north from where we are today. From the desert floor to the top of the mountain, at about 10,000 feet, we go through all of his six life zones, variable and blended as they are at their interfaces, and gradually cool off in the process.

A female black-headed grosbeak. Tucson, Arizona, August 1997.

CHAPTER 5

In Pursuit of Painted Redstarts and Red-faced Warblers in Arizona

ONE OF MY longest unfulfilled fantasies as a birder involved the painted redstart and red-faced warbler, two of the many Mexican migrants found in the mountains of southeastern Arizona. That desire was taken to another level early on by the publication in 1951 of Herbert Brandt's *Arizona and Its Bird Life*. Over a thirteen-year period, mostly in the 1940s, Brandt spent eight springs in southeastern Arizona. He studied the life histories of 170 species that nest in this one corner of Arizona, more than a quarter of the total breeding birds in North America at the time. Arizona claims about a dozen breeding warblers. This compares with New Hampshire's approximately twenty-four breeders. The two states share only three of these, the Nashville, yellow, and common yellow-throated warblers. When the Nature Conservancy bought the Ramsey Canyon Inn and 300 surrounding acres several years ago, the Huachuca Mountains were firmly imprinted as an eventual destination of mine.

Before getting down to the main business at hand, painted redstarts and red-faced warblers, I want to present some important background information on this wondrous state that has a significant bearing on the pursuit of these and other Arizona birds. On a typical July and August day in Tucson, monsoons, thunder, and lightning are often the primary topics of conversation. No matter what the purpose of a summer visit, weather will almost always intrude (perhaps the wrong word, because of the critical need of the monsoonal rains in the Southwest).

Nowhere have I seen such a display of natural fireworks on such a grand scale as in southeastern Arizona in midsummer. Each day usually starts with the famous sunshine, but by midmorning the familiar cumulus clouds quickly form and build into prodigious, billowing masses, colored with tints of blue and gray. In the afternoon these clouds darken to more ominous black and blue, presaging the climactic alchemies soon to turn the heavens into menacing maelstroms, dramatically changing day into evening. A variety of moods and thoughts sets in under these circumstances.

There, as far as the eye can see, across sprawling semidesert, nature's passion play unfolds: an endless variety of lightning dancing over the mountains, first here, then over there, and back again, some close together, others miles apart. I turn my head in every direction, awed by the tremendous intensity, the power, the energy, the beauty; I count the intervals between flashes—in seconds—to gauge how close or distant the lightning strikes are. Having heard about the monsoon season well ahead of time, I decide to pull off the road and sit out the worst of this in a truck stop on Interstate 10. We eventually make it back to the Holiday Inn in Tucson, unscathed and unswamped this time.

Every year, the worst of these thunderstorms suddenly turn dried-up washes (stream beds) into raging torrents across even downtown streets (there are few bridges in Tucson), sweeping everything with it, including vehicles whose drivers do not heed the warning signs to proceed no further until the rain stops and the flash flooding subsides enough to allow safe crossing. The passing of a flash flood can take anywhere from a few minutes to several hours, as Joseph Welch and I discovered one afternoon in the Patagonia–Sonoita Creek Preserve near the Mexican border. It was a most amazing experience. What looked like a harmless localized thunderstorm in the Patagonia Mountains several miles south of us soon turned the

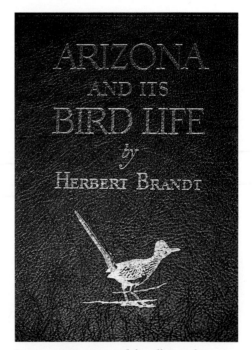

In my opinion, one of the all-time beautiful book covers: the 1951 Herbert Brandt classic, *Arizona and Its Bird Life*.

creek to flood stage, preventing further progress of our vehicle at a creek crossing. Luckily, there was an equally sudden appearance of a car and some Patagonia locals who saw our plight and escorted us to safety via an escape route.

These dramas are the most spectacular of all of nature's bag of beauties, but are best enjoyed undercover. On average, lightning kills nearly 100 people in the United States each year, more than any other weather event, including tornadoes. Some authorities cite Arizona and New Mexico as the thunderstorm capitals of the United States, whereas others say Florida leads in that notorious category. For more than an hour, I stand with my camera and telephoto lens at the sixth-floor window of our motel in Tucson, photographing the most dramatic and colorful orange, red, and yellow sunset-painted clouds, which form an

A sensational sunset over the Tucson Mountains after a typical summer monsoonal thunderstorm. Tucson, Arizona, August 1997.

unbelievable backdrop to the serrated Tucson Mountains on the western skyline of Tucson. People ask the question, "You're going to southern Arizona in August?" But the answer is obvious to a nature lover. The spectacular sunsets and awesome thunderstorms are a bonus, of course, depending on your viewpoint and fear index.

We are here primarily to attend the second annual North American Native Orchid Alliance meeting (15–18 August 1997). August is the best time for seeing and photographing a half dozen of Arizona's wild orchids. To do this, one must head for the mountains, the mighty Apache ranges in Cochise County, the last stronghold of Geronimo and his diehard band. There, an entirely different world awaits, thanks in part to the thunderstorms and the significant change in temperature and moisture each thousand feet produces in terms of vegetation and bird life.

The extreme Southwest's semidesert heat causes air to rise rapidly, which creates a partial vacuum and pulls up moist air from the Gulf of California, the eastern Pacific Ocean, and as far away as the Gulf of Mexico. This movement of moisture triggers almost daily thunderstorms, which account for more than 50 percent of the annual precipitation in Arizona and New Mexico. These storms, combined with the altitude, stimulate wild orchids and other vegetation to bloom. For every 1000-foot increase in elevation, temperature decreases by three to five degrees, which is the equivalent of driving 300 miles northward. In other words, at 8000 or 9000 feet in the Chiricahua Mountains of southeastern Arizona, just a stone's throw from the Mexican border, the climate is equivalent to that of boreal Canada. By the time you reach 8000 to 10,000 feet, the temperature is twenty degrees or so cooler and the vegetation is similar to the northern United States and southern Canada. On the way up, we drive through several other life zones, each with their own vegetational differences: Madrean pine/oak woodland, ponderosa pine forest, Douglas fir/aspen forest, and finally, the Hudsonian summit, where Engelmann spruce not only reaches its extreme southern limit in North America but is our southernmost spruce. Here also, of course, is where the most famous of the so-called Mexican bird element breeds in the United States.

Thousands of other birders have been attracted to these sky-island mountains over the years. The U.S. military began to arrive in the area in the 1850s; most of these parties had doctors and scientists as part of their team, many of whom were also avid birders eager to add to the knowledge of our expanding frontiers. Today, Arizona's annual economy is significantly blessed with the influx of birders and botanists. For anyone planning a trip to the sky islands, perhaps the best birding area in all of North America, I suggest Richard Cachor Taylor's *A Birder's Guide to Southeastern Arizona* (1995), the definitive guide for anyone making this expedition.

Taylor had this to say on the painted redstart: "This little jewel actually seems to come out to twist, turn, flutter and spread its outer tail-feathers as if to say, 'Look at me! Look at me!' If you give an owl call, you may get mobbed. You will undoubtedly see many of these flashing beauties, but you will never get to the point of saying, 'It's just a redstart.' Each one is too pretty and too animated to pass up." Herbert Brandt, on the other hand, while acknowledging "its outstanding feather combination and brilliant rhapsody of plumage," made the surprising statement that, "I personally can watch a redstart only so long, until my eyes become surfeited with its rich charms."

Both the painted redstart and the red-faced warbler are ground nesters in the mountains of Arizona. Ground nesting is not unusual with warblers—several eastern species such as the ovenbird and the black-and-white warbler also do it. But hole nesting is very unusual, with only the western Lucy's and the eastern prothonotary being habitual tree-cavity nesters. The painted redstart is the hardiest of the dozen or so species that breed in Arizona, returning to the snowy heights well before the end of March, well ahead of the red-faced. (Yes, the Santa Catalina Mountains, just northeast of Tucson, and those southeast, near the Mexican border, are frequently snow-covered in winter.) I used to think that southern Arizona was like southern California, coastal Texas, and Florida in winter, sunny and balmy with no snow, which is true for the most part in the valleys, but not the mountains.

After two days of searching with Joseph Welch, I am fortunate to see a single male redstart in Miller Canyon—sister canyon to the famed Ramsey Canyon of the Huachucas—at about 5000 feet in the Madrean pine/oak woodland, just above the manzanita and mountain mahogany habitat on the Miller Canyon Trail. (Most of my time on this trip is spent with orchids, with too little time for birds.) My companions on

Painted redstarts and a red-faced warbler. Painting by John Henry Dick, courtesy of the College of Charleston Foundation.

A painted redstart. Painting by George Miksch Sutton, courtesy of the University of Arizona Press.

this orchid field trip politely acknowledge my enthusiasm when I catch sight of the remarkable red, black, and white feathers, cavorting in typical redstart exuberance in the lower branches of an oak tree beside the trail, a few feet away from another amazing Arizona specialty, the alligator juniper, named for its remarkable "alligator hide" bark. The memory of that moment only reinforces a desire to repeat the experience on a grander scale, one exclusively devoted to birding.

Dr. Alexander Skutch (1973) described meeting three redstarts on their wintering grounds in Central America, our familiar American redstart, the Central American Kaup's redstart (*Myioborus miniatus*), and the painted redstart: "Later in the year, after the American redstarts came down from the north, I once encountered a single member of each of the three species foraging together in a little grove on the plateau near Tecpán. The American redstart was a male in perfect plumage. Since the sexes of the other two species are alike, it was impossible to decide whether they were male or female; but each was an excellent representative of its own kind. It was indeed difficult to judge which of the three was the most beautiful; but the painted redstart, with its deep, contrasting colors, most took my eye." It is of interest to note here that, until recently, the American redstart and painted redstart were considered very closely related and placed in the same genus, *Setophaga*, but now are separated, the painted placed in the much larger genus *Myioborus*. This change is based on such differences as the song and dimorphism (male and females have different colors) in *Setophaga* and the fact that the juvenal plumage of the young painted is retained much longer than that of the American redstart.

The red-faced warbler is a bird of the higher altitudes, above 7000 feet in the evergreen/aspen groves, a few thousand feet above the painted redstart, although their zones overlap somewhat. The red-faced warbler also usually forages higher in the trees than the painted. I am with my friends Ron Coleman and Joseph Welch on top of the Chiricahuas, near Rustler Park, at 8000 to 9000 feet. They wait about 100 yards lower on the trail while I photograph a pretty little purple *Malaxis* orchid. As soon as I do, I continue periodic scanning of the upper branches overhead and know instantly when the moment arrives: A flash of rose red flickers at the tip of a branch near the top of an Arizona pine. No other American warbler exhibits this flash of red on its head. While scrutinizing the dark green needles, the exquisitely exotic red-faced warbler keeps company with a veritable band of Mexican compatriots: the pretty yellow-throated Grace's warbler; the Mexican chickadee with gray sides and a larger black bib than our eastern chickadee; and the smallest of the lot, the gray-capped pygmy nuthatch (almost 2 inches smaller than the white-breasted).

The striking face of *Cardellina rubrifrons* is unlike anything else in the warbler clan, and fifty years of wishful—and sometimes wistful—thinking for this day is amply rewarded. Minutes later, I greet a reclining Ron and Joseph with the joyous news of discovery only to hear that they have also seen it while waiting patiently for my return, per-

A red-faced warbler. Photograph by Betty Darling Cottrille, courtesy of the Cornell Laboratory of Ornithology.

haps the same birding group in both instances. At any rate, my only regret is the brevity of the meeting. But that is the nature and challenge of birding—only rarely does one's cup runneth over, like Herbert Brandt's.

As I so often complain to anyone who listens, it is next to impossible to go birding and botanizing together successfully. Birding requires looking up, botanizing looking down on the ground, with the twain seldom meeting. Maybe next year I will have the opportunity—or take it, as Annie Dillard says—to spend a week with Joseph at the annual Sierra Vista Birding Festival in mid-August. More dreaming, perhaps, but life is all about hope.

CHAPTER 6

Hummingbird Heaven

WHICH ANIMAL has the highest metabolic rate of all? Most birders would probably guess the hummingbird, and they would be correct. I did not realize, however, that these tiny dynamos burn energy 100 times faster than the elephant. Hummingbirds have to consume their weight in nectar each and every day of their life to survive. Another fact I did not know: Hummingbirds are as small as any warm-blooded animal can be. Why? Because no animal would be able to eat enough food to maintain its body temperature (104°F) if it were smaller than the size of a hummingbird. So, why do hummingbirds rest so much? Are they conserving energy? That was the guess before scientists discovered otherwise. Although hummers burn energy eight times faster when they are hovering than when resting, during each hour of the feeding day hummingbirds actually feed for only about fifteen minutes, resting the other forty-five, according to ecologist Jared Diamond and others. The reason for this is that they are waiting for their stomach to partly empty the nectar and convert it into energy before the next bout of nectar gathering. (In addition to nectar, hummingbirds do eat other things: spiders and other insects like gnats, mosquitoes, and tree sap at woodpecker holes, which makes sense.) The interval between feedings is generally four minutes or so, which calculates to about fourteen or fifteen foraging trips every hour, each taking less than a minute.

Hummingbirds are also one of the few birds (along with swifts and poorwills) that can enter a torpid state at night, especially a cool night, to conserve energy. Their body temperature can fall to as much as fifty degrees below the normal daytime temperature. All of this explains

why hummingbirds—like many other birds—must head for the tropics in the autumn to survive. It also explains why year-round northern
residents must feed twenty times longer than they do in the summer
just to keep from freezing to death. Remember that fact the next time
someone questions the value of consistent winter feeding. Another
interesting observation: Sphinx moths, which look like hummingbirds
to the point of confusion, fly and hover at the same temperature as a
hummingbird in the warm months. However, because they are cold-
blooded, sphinx moths must survive the winter as eggs. In fact, adult
moths seldom live longer than a few weeks.

What's in a name? The magnificent hummingbird was formerly sad-
dled with the scientific and popular name of *rivoli* (derived from Victor Massena, the Duke of Rivoli in France). When it was discovered that
an earlier description of this hummingbird had priority, this name was
changed to magnificent (*fulgens*, which means "resplendent"), which is
far more appropriate. At just over 5 inches, the magnificent is the
largest hummingbird in the United States as well as one of the most
handsome, although not as brightly colored as some. A violet crown,
green gorget, and unusual black underparts present an overall and
unusual dark look. The size of the magnificent is closely followed by
another beauty, the blue-throated, which measures 5 inches. Having
said this, I must point out that some say the reverse is true: the blue-
throated is the largest. In either case the difference is a matter of a frac-
tion of an inch. The blue-throated hummingbird has the more common grayish underparts instead of the black of the magnificent, and,
of course, a blue, rather than green, throat. The smallest hummingbird in the United States is the calliope at 3.25 inches (it is also the
smallest bird in the United States), whereas the eastern ruby-throat is
closer to 4 inches.

The male of most hummingbird species has a brightly colored throat
(or gorget, as it is often called because of the scintillating metallic
reflections in sunlight), which is used for display purposes as well as
defending territory—usually prized flower patches. Hummingbirds are
so domineering around these flower patches that they will drive all
competitors away even to the point of tolerating a female only long
enough to mate. The gorgets may look black because of unfavorable
light or angle of view at any given moment, and that includes our east-

ern ruby-throated hummingbird. But patience pays off. One of the most common southwestern hummingbirds, the black-chinned, does have a partially black gorget, but the lower half is a pretty purple when the angle of light is just right.

At any time throughout the year in the extreme Southwest, there are about a dozen species, most of them visitors from Mexico and Central America taking advantage of the multitude of mountain flowers in the summertime and prolific numbers of nectar feeding stations a visitor sees everywhere. Most males of the hummingbird species are relatively easy to separate. All, except the broad-billed and violet-crowned, have dark bills. The broad-billed has the look of the blue-throated but in a much smaller (3.5 inches) body, whereas the violet-crowned is entirely white underneath with a violet crown. Both are easily distinguished in mixed company at any busy feeding station. The male Allen's and the male rufous are nearly identical except for the green back of Allen's. The hummingbird females, however, are an entirely different matter; look-alikes are more often the rule than the excep-

The luminescent gorget found in males of many hummingbird species is well displayed in this photograph of a rufous hummingbird. Rio Grande Nature Center, Albuquerque, New Mexico, early July 1994.

tion. Most females have gray or greenish sides, with the exception of the rufous and Allen's, which have buffy or rufous sides.

The hummingbird family numbers more than 320 species, all of which are confined to the Western Hemisphere, most of them in Central and South America. Of these, only 19 or 20 cross the Mexican border into the United States. Four nest as far north as Canada, with the rufous hummingbird ranging all the way to extreme southeastern Alaska. While other hummingbirds migrate through Mexico, following the bloom sequence of mountain flowers, the eastern ruby-throat makes the remarkable 600-mile nonstop flight across the Gulf of Mexico. The smallest of all hummers is the so-called Cuban bee hummingbird, which measures only 2.25 inches. The largest of all is the 8.5-inch giant hummingbird of the South American Andes Mountains, larger than the bluebird. Finally, in the "things you always wanted to know" category: Captive hummingbirds in zoos have lived to the ripe old age of ten to fifteen years.

Arizona is world famous for its hummingbirds because of its proxim-

A pair of black-chinned hummingbirds. Painting by Basil Ede, courtesy of Basil Ede and the Gulf States Paper Corporation.

ity to Mexico. It is possible to see fifteen species, with August probably the best of any month. Traditionally, the four best stations for hummingbirds have been the Spoffords' in Portal, the Patons' in Patagonia, Madera Canyon in the Santa Ritas, and Ramsey Canyon in the Huachucas, all within the sky islands of southeastern Arizona. A newcomer on the scene in the past ten years, Jesse Hendrix of Nogales, Arizona, a border town, apparently is the new hummingbird champion of the United States. According to a news feature in the *Arizona Star* mailed to me by my friend Joseph Welch of Tucson, Hendrix feeds up to 10,000 of these little dynamos every day. Steve Russell, a retired University of Arizona ornithologist, has been banding Hendrix's hummingbirds for the past five years, discovering among other things that the Santa Cruz Valley is a major migration route for these amazing birds.

Just as we Easterners perennially argue the pros and cons of winter feeding, apparently the same difference of opinion exists regarding hummingbird nectar feeders in the Southwest. And, as with winter feeding in general, there are more experts on the side of continuing the practice than stopping it. One expert believes that the hummingbirds are not pollinating as many flowers as usual, and, thus, artificial feeding is interfering with their life history. Others maintain that without tanking up on nectar in Arizona, many hummingbirds that fly through wide expanses of Mexican desert, where natural vegetation and wildflowers have been destroyed in favor of buffel grass for ranchers' cattle, perhaps would not survive.

All over the Southwestern landscape, one sees hummingbirds where there are wildflowers—along roadsides, mountain trails, and mountain meadows. But the most accessible species are at the backyard feeders, where Joseph Welch takes me on 12 August 1997. Our primary objectives are the Patons' backyard for hummingbirds and the Patagonia–Sonoita Creek Preserve, the latter purchased in 1966 by the Arizona chapter of the Nature Conservancy. Originally 312 acres in 1995, the preserve is now more than double that at 750 acres and hopefully still growing.

It is a very warm—make that hot—day as we travel east from Tucson on Interstate 10, then south on State Route 83. Off this stretch of road is one of the better places to see that clown of the bird world, the Montezuma quail (formerly known as Mearn's). In the 1960s researchers at the University of Arizona estimated a population of forty of these quail per square mile, and Richard Taylor (1995) believes that figure is still accurate today. While driving on Route 83, we are suddenly startled by a pair of small plump birds that flush up on the driver's side of the road. Joseph, who has absolutely no chance to avoid hitting one of them, lets out a yell: "Montezumas!" I ask, "Do you mind turning around so I can get a picture?" We both see that the male has taken the hit, the female escaping for another day. There is little traffic on this road, at least today, so we have no problem turning around to go back and pull over onto the road shoulder.

It is sad to see such a magnificent creature lying limp and lifeless on the gravel; Joseph, especially, is much more aware of their rarity than I am at this point. The calico black-and-white facial pattern, indeed the entire body, is magnificent and so different from any other bird: dark chestnut breast, extensive black sides with large uniform white spotting. What an amazing difference, though, between the dead bird in front of us and the animated glimpse a few seconds before, however brief. I think of how many hunters take pleasure in killing these remarkable New World quails, as the family Odontophoridae is called.

The ill-fated, clownish male Montezuma (or harlequin) quail. Sonoita, Arizona, August 1997.

(Formerly members of the grouse and pheasant family, quail have recently been separated into a family of their own based on new scientific evidence that emphasizes their chunky bodies and crested heads.) Then I remember their natural predators, like hawks, perhaps more onerous than the hunter, albeit part of the natural order. We wonder what prompted such sudden flushing. Perhaps the birds were not experienced with cars. Many birds in recent years, it appears to me at least, have learned to fly up and over oncoming traffic when they cross the road in flight.

The Montezuma quail certainly looks different, but it conjures up the equally handsome pattern of the harlequin duck, which I so often see on the coast of Maine each winter. In fact, the Montezuma quail is often referred to as the harlequin or fool quail. The latter appellation refers to this quail's habit of freezing rather than flushing on approach, relying almost entirely on camouflage. With such flamboyant coloration, it is easy to think that they must be "sitting ducks" without quickly flushing, but, on the contrary, the color combination is difficult to pick out in the lights and shadows among the grasses, and the male quail knows it.

The harlequin quail's habitat is quite specific: open savannah-like grasslands with scattered oaks and pines. It has a very restricted distribution: in the southeastern corner of Arizona, a narrow strip in southwestern New Mexico, and an even smaller arc in the Big Bend of southwestern Texas. Although holding its own in a few of the remotest areas, the future does not bode well for this extraordinary bird. Livestock overgrazing (with the emphasis on *over*) and summer droughts appear to be the two most limiting factors in the year-to-year population fluctuations of this species. Currently, there are no management parameters in place that would help to stabilize the remaining numbers of the Montezuma quail. For an excellent account of this bird, read Julie Hagelin's piece in *Birding Magazine* (October 1998). Feast your eyes on the color photography of R. D. Wilberforce and Rob Curtis—the best I've seen.

The thought of this unexpected encounter stays with me the rest of the way to Sonoita, even as we stop a few minutes later to scan the grasslands for pronghorn antelope, with no success. Once at the Patons', there is no room in my mind to dwell further on the quail, with hummingbirds feasting the brain for the next hour or more. We tick off five species here, despite the midday sun's heat. Apparently the well-shaded feeders under the trees keep the hummingbirds interested all day. The broad-billed is the most abundant while we watch, followed by the black-chinned. Anna's and rufous are also here. But the main attraction is the violet-crowned hummingbird. According to Richard Taylor (1995), the Patons' backyard is the most dependable site for it in all of the United States. He also says that the Patons hosted the only visit of the cinnamon hummingbird in the United States in July 1992. But the blue-throated and magnificent hummingbirds are never seen here (except in winter) because they prefer the cooler temperatures near the top of the 9000-foot Santa Catalinas' coniferous forest, northeast of Tucson. On another day with our fellow orchid enthusiast Ron Coleman, we watch the blue-throated and magnificent hummingbirds at yet another feeding station, while eating lunch in an outdoor cafe in the Catalinas. We are literally only a few feet away from touching them, the birds so used to humans walking past constantly. This scene was more enjoyable than the meal itself, and it more than made up for the interminably slow service.

After leaving the Patons', Joseph Welch and I head to the Nature Conservancy Preserve, which, unfortunately, is closed today. We decide to walk the gravel road beside the creek instead. Joseph hears a gray hawk in the large, broken-down sycamores that line the creek. The trees appear to have experienced a certain amount of storm damage, or perhaps it is merely natural old age. Whatever the reason, the birding is good, again despite the heat of the day. We see Bewick's wren, black phoebe, bridled titmouse, MacGillivray's and yellow warblers (the former perhaps an early migrant), tropical kingbird, and several others not certainly identified. It is now late in the afternoon, after earlier thunderstorms in distant mountains—only a sprinkle on us—cause Sonoita Creek to transform from a shallow, placid, barely moving stream to a raging flood tide, almost stranding us for hours. As I mentioned in chapter 5, we were saved from floating away by some locals.

On the hottest of days, Joseph Welch turns up ever more new birds with little effort, walking the streets of northeast Tucson. A handsome male vermilion flycatcher appears even more listless than we are under the searing sun. An early migrating male Wilson's warbler is a surprise to me, as is the frequency of the northern cardinal, which also breeds in Texas and Mexico, but only in extreme southern Arizona and New Mexico in the West. We see a pyrrhuloxia, which resembles a cardinal: gray all over except for a red face, red tip of the crest, touches of red on the wings, tail, and underparts, and a distinctive yellow bill. Even the song is different: not as strong, shorter, and lower-scaled than the northern cardinal. The ubiquitous cactus wren, house sparrow, Cooper's hawk, mourning dove, and white-winged dove round out the morning here on the streets of the newest suburb of ever-expanding Tucson, whose population climbs steadily to more than a half million inhabitants.

A side trip to White Sands National Monument in southwestern New Mexico—well worth the long ride—includes a stop at Little Florida Mountain at Rockhound State Park in Deming, New Mexico, where the black-throated sparrow, canyon wren, and curve-billed thrasher

The almost ubiquitous cactus wren building its nest. Arizona-Sonora Desert Museum, Tucson, Arizona, 30 July 1997.

(the most common desert thrasher, of which there are several species in the Southwest), alternately sing and sulk. This rather strange and unusual state park is located on the side of a rock-strewn mountain with several trails for rock hounding. Nobody was around, except for a German couple higher up the trail. Besides the birds and wildflowers, their object and ours is the rocks, mostly composed of jasper, a member of the quartz group of minerals, which includes agates, amethyst, rock crystal, chalcedony, and petrified wood. Jasper is usually streaked or spotted, most often a dull dark red or brown, and used mostly for ornamental objects and cabochons (a plain cut stone with flat bottom and rounded top). As often is the case, this area is well picked over with little of interest—unless one wishes to climb, which we are not on this very hot morning.

The black-throated sparrow is a common resident sparrow of southern New Mexico and Arizona, requiring only a rocky slope, some cholla cacti (*Opuntia*), and other cacti brush along a dried-up wash. As Phillips et al. say in *The Birds of Arizona* (1964), it is the desert sparrow "par excellence." In fact, the bird's former name is desert sparrow. But the newer name is more appropriate, for it truly is a handsome bird: large triangular black throat and face that contrast nicely with pure white eyebrow (supercilium), white malar patch below the face, and large expanse of white underparts. Its tinkling, musical song is frosting on the cake.

At high noon on the hottest day of our visit in Tucson, we watched the cactus wren, the state bird of Arizona and one of the very few things still stirring under the stifling noontime sun. The cactus wren is as large as a starling, believe it or not, and almost as ubiquitous in the Lower Sonoran zone of southern Arizona and New Mexico. The bird's presence is easily noted in these favored sites, both by its loud, churring *cha, cha, cha* song and its conspicuous nest. The nest is bulky and very disheveled, often half hanging out of a cholla cactus bush, loose ends blowing in the hot breezes, as if the bird is saying "Here it is, come and get it." Apparently, the cactus wren has little concern for predators because of the thorny site of its nest. Two of the best places to view the cactus wren up close and personal are at the Arizona-Sonora Desert Museum just west of Tucson and the Saguaro National Park, the western division of which is nearby the museum and the

The magnificent saguaro (*Carnegiea gigantea*), a tree-sized cactus, is the state flower of Arizona and is symbolic of the American Southwest. This cactus grows only in the Sonoran Desert of southern and southwestern Arizona, extreme southeastern California, and northern Sonora, Mexico. Tucson, Arizona, August 1997.

eastern section of which is east of Tucson. Many other Sonoran Desert birds are here also, some captive in the outdoor museum and others wild among the most fascinating plants you will ever want to see, including the saguaro cactus, certainly one of the highlights of a trip that should not be missed.

CHAPTER 7

The Land of the Roadrunner

THE MEXICANS call this bird *el paisano* (meaning "country-man"), an endearing term for one whose presence brings good fortune to the household, or *corre camino* ("runs the road"). In Texas, it is known as lizard-eater and snake-eater. To the rest of us—at least the birders and especially the cartoonists and their followers—this bird is the equally beloved roadrunner of the southwestern deserts, ranging from Texas to California and Mexico. To me and many others, the roadrunner symbolizes the Southwest, as does the saguaro. Whereas the former can be seen throughout the Southwest, the latter is restricted to the Sonoran Desert (west of the eastern outskirts of Phoenix and Tucson and southwest of Prescott, Arizona, as well as south into Mexico). When I saw my first live examples of the road-runner in Albuquerque and the saguaro in Tucson, I was thoroughly impressed. My wife, Susan, first whetted an appetite for the Southwest, having made trips there to visit a sister and fallen in love with the red sandstones and sprawling vistas. As much as I admired the red rocks and open spaces, however, I fell in love with el paisano and the largest cactus in the United States.

The roadrunner is almost 2 feet long and has three features that stand out: the heavy bill; bushy crest; and, especially, the long, mobile tail. The bird's usual gait is to run forward with all parts on a more or less horizontal plane, perfectly simulating the cartoon caricature, then stop suddenly to look around for the things a roadrunner looks for, notably insects, lizards, and snakes. The tail comes into action when the object of his pursuit is cornered or at least within striking distance, at which point, it acts as brake, rudder, and balancer all in one motion.

Although the roadrunner's actions appear comical (the bird is a member of the cuckoo family, after all), this activity is all business and purpose in its daily desire to stay alive and perpetuate the species. It is interesting to note that the main characteristic of the cuckoo family is the structure of the feet: two front toes pointing forward and two rear toes pointing backward. This creates the proverbial "X marks the spot" in the dirt, while making it impossible to determine in which direction the bird has gone.

The Pueblo Indians of New Mexico—some of the earliest birders, by the way—took advantage of this riddle in the sand by placing roadrunner tracks (essentially Xs) around their domiciles to confuse the evil spirits of the dead. They also revered the bird for its strength and courage in battling the rattlesnake. The roadrunner is no dummy, however. If the rattlesnake puts up a concerted defense, the bird will usually just walk away from the fray. It also chooses to do battle only with rattlers less than 2 feet in length. But when it does throw down the

The unique roadrunner, king of the desert. Albuquerque, New Mexico, July 1994.

gauntlet, it usually wins by a combination of guile and remarkable lightning-fast footwork, striking the snake behind the head with its powerful bill and snapping it against the ground until it gives up the ghost. El paisano then leisurely swallows it whole, and it can take a good deal of time for the digestive juices to do their job.

In early July 1994, we spend three wonderful days at the Rio Grande Nature Center State Park (the area's best-kept secret) just a few minutes from downtown Albuquerque, New Mexico. Talk about the comforts of home—this is the place. For hours on end, I relax on plush couches while watching dozens of black-chinned hummingbirds cavorting back and forth around several well-placed nectar feeders just beyond large plate-glass windows. The windows keep the hot, dry air on the outside while the air-conditioned fresh air on the inside enhances the amazingly animated entertainment outside. Later in the month when the hummers begin to migrate, three newcomers will join the black-chins: the broad-tailed (a look-alike of the eastern ruby-throated); the gorgeous rufous with the orange gorget; and the diminutive calliope, the smallest North American hummingbird, with the unique straight, black (in some, light red) moustache. I alternately read, rest, watch at

Hummingbirds at Albuquerque's Rio Grande Nature Center. July 1994.

A broad-tailed hummingbird and red penstemon (*Penstemon cardinalis*), one of its favorite sources of nectar in New Mexico's drylands. Painting by Cindy Nelson-Nold, courtesy of the artist.

my own speed, and spend several hours photographing, taking notes, and listening to knowledgeable local birders conversing on the latest arrivals. Then I walk through the woods to a tranquil backwater of the Rio Grande, where hundreds of black-chinned hummingbirds fly back and forth over the calm water (fly-catching like swallows often do, under different circumstances). The soil is powder dry and the vegetation reflects this, with only the spiny silverleaf nightshade *Solanum elaeagnifolium*, which is well adapted to drought, bearing a full complement of broadly five-pointed purple flowers laden with dust.

All the other birds keep close to the manmade lake in front of the observation bunker, a low structure that blends so well with its surroundings that one does not see it until suddenly coming upon the steel tunnel entrance, actually a very large culvert, unlike anything I have seen architecturally. A Gambel's quail feeds with great-tailed grackles and red-winged blackbirds on a wooden platform feeder beside the water, while dozens of wood ducks, in all stages of molt, listlessly glide over the water, dirtied by the molted feathers and excrement. Some ducks also escape the heat by dozing in shaded coves. And, of course, the roadrunners do their thing, the heat of midday notwithstanding. Three of them cavort around the parking lot, maintaining just enough distance as I attempt to photograph them for an hour. Roadrunners rarely fly, but are perfectly able, relying on their great agility and speed on the ground instead. They can easily outrun me, but not a horse, as was once thought. The roadrunner has been clocked at about 15 miles per hour, about half as fast as most horses, but three times faster than me.

A book with the most amazing photographs of the roadrunner—or any other bird, for that matter—was written and photographed by Wyman Meinzer, a native Texan, chosen by *Sports Afield* as one of the top outdoor photographers in 1985. Meinzer's *The Roadrunner* (1993) is a remarkable collection of roadrunner photographs.

With the possible exception of southeastern Arizona, which has more species, the hours spent at the Rio Grande Nature Center remain the grandest of all my hummingbird experiences. At nearby Petroglyph National Monument, on the western outskirts of Albuquerque, residential development encroaches to the very borders of the park, emphasizing the explosive growth (with a population of more than

600,000) that continues here and in other parts of the Southwest. Our friend the roadrunner could care less, at the moment anyway, as he scurries ahead of us, a lizard transfixed in his bill, speeding to a nearby nest of five nestlings. The ranger revealed the nest's existence on our inquiry, while refusing to divulge the location.

A few minutes later we encounter the largest snake I have ever seen, a remarkable cream, tan, and chestnut–colored, 6- to 8-foot bull snake, which looks like a brightly patterned rattlesnake. There are eleven species of rattlesnakes in Arizona and New Mexico, all poisonous. It is wise to take certain precautions, some obvious but worth a reminder. For example, 50 to 75 percent of snakebites occur because the person is trying to kill, capture, or harass a snake. One should avoid rock crevices and ledges and be cautious while traversing grassy-shrubby areas, where snakes often take refuge from the heat of the day. Although more apt to be active at night and on cloudy days, snakes are nevertheless often seen in the heat of the day, as we experienced several times in the Southwest. Incidentally, making incisions at the point of the bite is now discouraged by most authorities. It is better to use a

The cover of the definitive book on the species, *The Roadrunner* (1993) by Wyman Meinzer. Courtesy of Texas Tech University Press.

vacuum pump directly on the bite—ideally within three minutes—and transport the victim as quickly as possible to the nearest health care facility, which is reason enough to have a companion along on any excursion. Of course, the ideal circumstances do not often occur. In those cases, however, it is important to get to a hospital as quickly as possible.

George Miksch Sutton (1980), the famous Oklahoma artist, teacher, and author, described the mystique of the one who runs the road: "Most ornithologists are to some extent acquainted with the roadrunner. But he who really knows him has risen morning after morning with the desert sun; thrilled at the brilliance of the desert stars; seen day turned to sudden night by the dust-storm; pulled cactus spines from his shins. He who knows the roadrunner, he who has measured the breadth and the depth of this unique bird personality, has lived with him—not for an hour or so, not for a day, but week after week after week." Wyman Meinzer has done that, and almost forty years earlier Beula-Mary Wadsworth penned the following lines in her poem "To a Roadrunner" (1964):

> Run, pert cock o' the desert,
> Funny old friendly bird
> Bright speckled feathers
> And "kook-kook" word;
> Rudder-tail a-veering
> Your crooked neck held out,
> Run, quick feet, and follow trails
> Where lizard and cricket scout.
> Eyes alert go chase it,
> Go race a car or truck,
> Run, have fun, and happy day
> But stay near my home for luck.

Both Sutton and Wadsworth pretty well sum up the story of the roadrunner.

CHAPTER 8

Brazos Bend State Park, Texas

I

T'S NOT Aransas National Wildlife Refuge, Santa Ana National Wildlife Refuge, Laguna-Atacosta National Wildlife Refuge, Sabal Palm, Pedro Island—all lower Texas coast hot spots—or even High Island on the upper coast southeast of Houston, but it could be one of the best-kept secrets in Texas birding. I am referring to Brazos Bend State Park, an easy 50-mile ride southwest of Houston on Interstate 59. We drive past acres and acres of former cotton fields that are now surveyed and landscaped for the inevitable and accelerated expansion of metropolitan Houston (now the fourth largest city in the United States), with huge billboards announcing one development after another. Mile after mile, I see nothing else and wonder when and where it is all going to end, knowing full well that it probably never will. Will the development eventually even catch up with Brazos Bend, maybe within the next decade or two? This is a depressing question, as is the ride out of Houston, until finally the signs stop. I turn off I-59 and head south along State Route 762, which is still lined with cattle, cotton, barbed-wire fences, and fence posts occasionally displaying the magnificent scissor-tailed flycatcher, the "Texas bird of paradise." At this point I temporarily forget the distressing potential of urban sprawl that preoccupied my mind just minutes before.

As I slow down for a better view, the graceful scissor-tail lifts off the fence post to glide like an angel to the next post, then sallies forth to catch a grasshopper or other insect morsel. The subtle beauty of the soft pearl gray head, breast, shoulders, and back contrasts with the bright salmon pink and white underparts and wing linings. But that's not all: Trailing behind is the spectacular 9-inch black-and-white tail

A scissor-tailed flycatcher from the classic *The Bird Life of Texas* (1974) by Harry Oberholser. Painting by Louis Agassiz Fuertes, courtesy of the University of Texas Press.

that opens and closes like a scissors. This bird is truly an apparition from heaven if there ever was one. The total length of the bird is about 14 inches. What a fabulous addition to my life list.

Earlier in the morning of this sixtieth consecutive scorching Texas day, on the balcony of our son's apartment in Houston, I admire another gray Texan on its leisurely journey to South America, a dozen of them sailing on thermals back and forth, up and down, catching their breakfast of moths and other insects that still cruise above the big cities. With black wings and tail, the Mississippi kite looks very dark from below except for its head, which is very pale gray—almost white. The good news is that this kite is actually increasing across the southern plains, when other species are declining. Tree planting for windbreaks and erosion control may be providing more nesting sites for the Mississippi kite. It is a strange feeling to watch these raptors beginning their migration, which will continue for several more weeks, in such hot weather of mid-August. Our oldest son is in his first job, as a research mathematician at Rice University, his wife a clinical social worker at the Methodist Hospital. We are here for the birth of our first grandchild, Kaitlin Emily Keenan. You cannot get much happier than that.

Cattle egrets are everywhere in the pastures and fields; it has been thirty years or more since this egret paid a visit to New Hampshire for a few summers before deciding to head back to where there are far more cattle. These birds are the size of snowy egrets and have buffy tan feathers on the head, shoulders, and breast. Cattle egrets are immigrants from Africa that arrived in Florida in the 1950s, proving once again that the United States is the land of opportunity for birds as well as human beings. As their name implies, cattle egrets are commonly associated with cows and other cattle, catching insects disturbed by the movements of the herd. The birds even follow farm machinery, for the same reason, defending them as territory, just as they do the cattle. This is a strange sight indeed, but so commonplace down here. This egret can now be seen over half of the United States, even into southernmost Canada, but is uncommon in most areas.

We are now inside Brazos Bend State Park with the family, driving to the main attractions at Half Lake, Elm Lake, Pilant Lake, and Forty-Acre Lake. The largest is Elm Lake, where I am startled by the 2-foot-wide circular leaves of the American lotus (*Nelumbo lutea*), which have petioles (leaf stems) attached underneath at the very center. The resulting effect is like moving umbrellas or waving elephant ears a foot above the water. Even the yellow flowers, which resemble water lilies, are nearly a foot in diameter. The American lotus is common in parts of Louisiana, Mississippi, and eastern Texas, but few other places. I have never seen such a strange plant as this, a reminder of the lush tropics. The spectacle covers a good portion of the lake and almost eclipses some other attractions nearby, like the flock of gorgeous roseate spoonbills, the pink flamingo to Texans, too far away to really appreciate without binoculars. I also notice a king-sized alligator, up close and personal, with some of her babies (only a few inches in length) riding comfortably on her broad armored back under the interested gaze of several spectators just a few feet away. I left the camera back in the

Water hyacinths (*Eichhornia crassipes*) in Brazos Bend State Park, Texas, southwest of Houston. 24 April 1995.

car, and, despite the prompting of my family, decide not to go back and get it, feeling that she and the babies will not still be around when I return. But they would have been: a golden opportunity missed. The alligators are so common and tame here that some people are tempted to aggravate them—with regret—despite the warning signs.

Mississippi kites and prothonotary warblers breed at Brazos, but both have departed earlier in the month. (It is a surprise to me that so many southern birds actually finish their breeding duties, pack up, and leave earlier than some of our northern breeders.) Black-bellied whistling-ducks are one of the Texas prizes we do see, however, more than thirty sitting alert in the marshy area across from the visitor center. Several dozen nest here in boxes erected for their specific use. Their bright red bills and feet, white eye-rings surrounding black eyes, and gray face and head exclaim as loudly as their clarion whistles do. A rusty body and black belly and tail complete the distinctive, yet handsome look of this tropical Middle American duck. Male and female black-bellied whistling-ducks form long-term bonds, but, as John Tveten (1993) describes it, "in spite of this fidelity, females sometimes

An alligator in Brazos Bend State Park, Texas. Photograph taken with a 400-mm telephoto. 27 April 1994.

lay their eggs in other nests, 'dump nests' containing up to 100 eggs, the product of several females' thwarted instincts." The sweltering heat on this day has kept most of the human population at home and some of the wild natives under cover. But enough are performing their daily duties while we sweat and drink from our own water supply. White ibises, purple gallinules, tricolored and little blue herons, a yellow-crowned night-heron, and anhingas are in evidence, as well as many ducks and the ubiquitous coots, the strange bird "with the body and habits of a duck, the bill of a chicken, the lobed toes of a grebe, and the family lineage of the rails and gallinules," as John Tveten describes them in his excellent *The Birds of Texas* (1993). One yellow-crowned night-heron posed indefinitely for me, as the accompanying picture shows, literally not moving for what seemed like a half hour. The trees have their complement of birds, but there is not enough time to spend with the new songs and sounds.

The red-bellied woodpecker announces itself by rolling *churrr* calls. This truly beautiful woodpecker (misnamed for a slight red wash on the belly) is noted for the extremely handsome combination of scarlet

A white ibis. Brazos Bend State Park, Texas, 27 April 1994.

top and back of head, as well as a black-and-white barred back and tail. The red-bellied is quite common here and apparently is extending its range north into New England. Another member of the clan confined to western Texas and equally misnamed, the golden-fronted wood-pecker, should be called the "golden-naped," because that is where the conspicuous golden orange color is located, the belly being merely tinged with yellow. The golden-fronted woodpecker also has the zebra back pattern, as do many of the twenty-two members of the Picidae, but none more beautifully than the red-bellied.

Brazos Bend State Park contains nearly 5000 acres and is located on the banks of the Brazos River, which was a major commerce route for cotton in the mid-1800s. The park lies in what is known as the Brazos bottomlands, or floodplains. A tributary called Big Creek meanders through the park. Both are lined with sycamores, cottonwoods, and black willows; live oaks festooned with Spanish moss, burr oaks, water oaks, and pecans are part of the bottomland hardwood forest. One of the top attractions for me in this park is its remarkable flora, amateur botanist that I am. In addition to the American lotus, another favorite

A close-up profile of a yellow-crowned night-heron. Photograph taken with a 400-mm telephoto. Brazos Bend State Park, Texas, 27 April 1994.

is the so-called celestial iris or prairie nymph (*Herbertia lahue* subsp. *caerulea*, also known simply as herbertia), which covers the grass on the way to the black-bellied whistling-ducks. Endemic to eastern Texas and western Louisiana, this exquisitely fragile iris suffers from a lack of official identity in the halls of the taxonomist, but not from a lack of beauty. In prime condition, 2-inch bluish violet flowers on 6-inch stems originating from a perennial bulb carpet the ground, until a sudden downpour obliterates the ultrathin tepals (sepals and petals), washing out the delicate colors. Meadow pinks (*Sabatia campestris*), or prairie rose-gentian (a member of the gentian family), is another blooming beauty. The unusual Turk's-cap (*Malvaviscus arboreus* var. *drummondii*), a woody 3-foot-tall mallow, sports 1-inch red partially closed mallow flowers, with typically projecting stamen columns. All under a searing sun of mid-August. I love it.

In addition to Brazos Bend, this tremendous state has so much more going for it that I have yet to experience. In southern coastal Texas, Roger Tory Peterson noted, "it is possible to see more birds in a day than any other section of the United States." During January through April, the best place to be is the region between Rockport and Brownsville. Year in, year out, Santa Ana, Laguna-Atacosta, and Aransas National Wildlife Refuges produce more birds than any other national wildlife refuges in the country. Then there is High Island further up the coast and the Big Thicket in the piney woods of eastern Texas, once the home of the most famous but now sadly extinct ivory-billed woodpecker, a bird that I discuss in chapter 21.

Herbertia lahue subsp. *caerulea*, popularly known as the celestial iris, is an intensely beautiful but fragile native Texan. Photograph taken with a 100-mm macro lens. Brazos Bend State Park, Texas, 27 April 1994.

CHAPTER 9

Florida Folly

I N 1999 in the Everglades, the state of Florida and the federal government initiated the world's largest ecological restoration program. President Clinton asked for $282 million to fund the restoration, which involves the reestablishment of vital water levels in the magnificent wetlands of southern Florida. In 2001 Congress approved funding for the project.

The Everglades are part of the tremendous 14,000-square-mile watershed that begins around Lake Okeechobee (meaning "big water") and flows ever so gradually to the Gulf of Mexico 300 miles to the south. Think of it as a tremendous but shallow saucer of water, 100 miles long and roughly 50 miles wide, with a mere 10-foot change of elevation from the highest (Bok Tower) to lowest point (sea level). The saucer is composed of coral and oolitic limestone. Everglades National Park, located just a few miles southwest of the sprawling metropolis of Miami, was established in 1947. It is extremely difficult to fathom the logic of what happened next.

Beginning that very same year, 1800 miles of canals were built to drain this unique wetland over a period of years for the sake of giant sugar companies and the U.S. Army Corps of Engineers. Politicians pandering to the sugar industry in Florida are the main cause of the disruption of water flow from Lake Okeechobee to the Everglades. Those who engineered this redirection of water by locks and canals and the sugar companies who polluted the precious water resources with fertilizer and pesticide runoff are the responsible parties, and the facts are clear on the matter. How did they do it? By lobbying Congress and the president of the United States, as well as state government, since the

1940s. In fact, we taxpayers subsidize this sugar production because world prices are lower than Florida businesses can meet.

Today, hopefully, the tide is beginning to turn, thanks in a major way to the indefatigable Marjorie Stoneman Douglas, Florida's leading environmental activist, who died in May 1998 at the ripe old age of 108. To quote the remarkable Douglas: "There are no other Everglades in the world. They are, they have always been, one of the unique regions of the earth." Water is what Florida is all about. There are 1700 rivers and streams in the state; more than 7000 lakes and ponds; and, most importantly, 300 major springs. These underground water depositories (aquifers) are moving all the time, albeit slowly. The most important one, called the Floridian aquifer, begins in South Carolina and flows beneath the entire peninsula of Florida, through a vast network of limestone that underlies most of the state. Winter cold-front rains and summer thunderstorms, which produce an average rainfall of 60 inches annually, replenish this precious water. However, human consumption, a reflection of Florida's tremendous population explosion, especially in the 1950s and 1960s, is causing these aquifers to shrink, even dry up, along with some lakes and ponds. Experimentation with desalinization continues in certain areas, but the cost is three times that of freshwater sources—the main drawback at this point. Water and land once were cheap in Florida, but no longer. The clock is ticking.

I took my first trip to Florida in late March and early April 1955. That was my only visit until some forty-four years later, in April 1999. Entire books have been written on the subject of change throughout the state. The proverbial snowbirds from the North are one reason for the huge environmental devastation that has transformed a once subtropical paradise into nonstop wall-to-wall development. The unending influx of retirees requires support of a necessary infrastructure that is equally overwhelming. I was amazed in April 1999 to see what is happening in the city of Naples on the southwestern coast, for example. Only a few years ago, the Naples area was one of the last remaining wild areas in the state. The main thoroughfare—Interstate 41—now requires more than a half-hour ride from the south end to the north side of the city because of new construction. It is only a matter of time before a new bypass will be necessary to relieve this creep and crawl.

There are oases, of course, scattered here and there throughout the state, mostly in the form of state parks and three notable national forests in the northern half of the state: Apalachicola, south of Tallahassee in the panhandle of Florida, is the largest of the three (558,000 acres), followed by Ocala National Forest (382,000 acres) and Osceola National Forest (179,000 acres). Apalachicola is noted for carrying the largest population of red-cockaded woodpeckers (1500 birds in 1993) in the world. The three forests are also noted for their brown-headed nuthatches, Bachman's sparrows, and pine warblers. In 1993, Ocala National Forest was home to the second largest population of Florida scrub-jays in the world.

We are fortunate, too, to have the three national parks in extreme southern Florida, as well as national preserves and national wildlife

A ride before sunset along the Route 1A shore drive. Palm Beach, Florida, 7 April 1955.

refuges. In addition to the Everglades National Park, there is Biscayne Bay National Park and Dry Tortugas National Park. Add another four national wildlife refuges, two national preserves, and several state parks and preserves, and the picture is improving, as long as national and state funding increases, which it has not been in the past several years. In fact, the opposite has occurred, and the park system is in jeopardy as I write—thus, the dire need for Congress and the state legislature to finally do what is right for Florida and the nation.

In addition to Everglades National Park, outstanding remnants of Florida's magnificent and unique subtropical forests and swamps include the nearly 800,000-acre Big Cypress National Preserve, the 26,000-acre Florida Panther National Wildlife Refuge, and the 62,000-acre Fakahatchee Strand State Preserve (a strand is a long and narrow swamp that is usually underwater, but filled with subtropical trees and other vegetation). For obvious reasons, the public is allowed only limited access to these preserves, especially the panther refuge. The Fakahatchee is considered—by some people at least—to be one of the most dangerous places in all of Florida to travel without a guide. It is also the protected home of some outstanding, mostly tiny, wild orchids that include the magnificent frog orchid (*Coeloglossum viride* var. *virescens*), which blooms in the hottest part of the summer. The Fakahatchee is home to the largest stand (5000) of native or naturally growing (as opposed to the cultivated specimens seen in cities) royal palms. Unfortunately, few virgin bald cypress remain in the Big Cypress because of clear-cutting in the 1940s. Thanks to the foresight of the Norris family, however, 215 acres at Big Bend, just off I-41 near the southwestern corner of Big Cypress Preserve, can still be admired by the public. Two of the best publications on these areas are Tim Ohr's *Florida's Fabulous Natural Places* (1999) and Bill Pranty's *A Birder's Guide to Florida* (1996).

Now, to the birding: In the southern half of the state, the privately owned Corkscrew Swamp Sanctuary, saved by the National Audubon Society in 1954, consists of more than 10,000 acres and contains the largest and oldest stand of bald cypress. The name is derived from the fact that the trees are deciduous and drop their needles each autumn, becoming bald in the winter. A 2.25-mile boardwalk takes the visitor through wet prairie, pond cypress swamp, and then the big beautiful bald cypress swamp. The day we visit reflects the severe drought plaguing most of the state in 1998 and early 1999: dried-up and shriveled resurrection ferns along with most other things, but the bromeliads (*Tillandsia*) are in relatively good shape, the sharply pointed colored bracts glistening in occasional shafts of afternoon sunlight, making for a great photographic opportunity. The tremendous load of plants carried by these magnificent bald cypress are normally beautiful in their own right and transform the trees into garlands of fresh color, but, sadly for us, not this spring.

The state has proposed acquiring additional land surrounding the sanctuary as part of the Corkscrew Regional Watershed project. Again, though, while driving State Route 846 eastward away from the park, I

A sweltering-hot green heron. Corkscrew Swamp, Naples, Florida, 14 April 1999.

see nothing but new housing developments for dozens of miles, sprinkled here and there with giant nurseries that supply the constant demand for landscape-size trees and shrubs to decorate the new artificial landscape. If you want to feel disheartened, go to Florida and see what is happening. While on this subject, I'll mention the monocultural orange plantations, mile after mile as far as the eye can see, which I saw fifty years ago in the central part of the state, north of Okeechobee, and still see today.

The water table is so low during my visit that most of the birds and alligators concentrate in the few surviving water holes, such as the so-called lettuce lakes. Alligators, with several babies swimming close to their mothers, boom occasionally, as does an American bittern from the distant marshes: *oonk-a-lunk, oonk-a-lunk*, sounding like pipes sucking up deep mud. Whether the bittern breeds here is a question that Audubon caretakers are still trying to solve for certain. Documented accounts of nesting American bitterns are sketchy at best, and the park's staff is always interested in hearing about these *oonk-a-lunk* calls in April. Wood storks usually nest here, if the water level cooperates, which it does not this year. A few are flying around today, however, including one that momentarily perches on the boardwalk railing, although it does not sit long enough for my camera. Purple gallinule, little blue heron, glossy ibis, American egret, and snowy egret are some

A green anole, Florida's most common lizard. Corkscrew Swamp, Naples, Florida, 14 April 1999.

An alligator along the boardwalk in the National Audubon Society's Corkscrew Sanctuary. Collier County, Florida, 14 April 1999.

of the other birds I see. Despite the disappointing effects of the drought, I have a fascinating six hours here, which could easily extend the entire day, but traveling to and from Corkscrew does not allow any more precious time.

Highlands Hammock State Park near Sebring, consisting of more than 5000 acres, is one of the best of all Florida state parks. Southwest of this park lies a tract of swamp that the state is considering purchasing; the swamp has the unfortunate distinction of being the last place a verified sighting of ivory-billed woodpeckers occurred in North America (1968). On our visit, however, an almost equally captivating and larger bird (2 feet long and 4-foot wingspan) performs for us: a marvelous gyrating swallow-tailed kite. Elliot Coues, one of America's great early ornithologists, described the bird's flight as "like a trained gymnast under marvelous control," breathtaking in contrasting snow white and crow black. Magnificent is the only word for the swallow-tailed kite, unsurpassed in beauty and elegance and quite accessible, often flying close to the ground—unlike the Mississippi kite. The swallow-tail nests in Highlands Hammock Park regularly and can be seen flying just above the trees from March through July. According to Bill Pranty (1996), an estimated 1000 to 3000 birds are summer residents of Florida, which represents the majority of the U.S. population.

Arthur Cleveland Bent, in his classic *Life Histories of North American Birds* (1937), tells of his first experience with this kite, a practice that is thankfully a thing of the distant past:

> We saw seven of these lovely birds sailing about over the prairie. They seemed to be quartering the ground systematically in the search for prey. It was a joy to watch their graceful movements and a pity to disturb them, but my companion, the late Louis A. Fuertes, and I both wanted specimens. We concealed ourselves in the long grass and had not long to wait before we had two of the birds down on the ground and five others hovering over them, after the manner of terns, uttering their weak squealing notes. We shot no more; they were too beautiful; and we were rapt in admiration of their gracefulness, the purity of their contrasting colors, and the beautiful grapelike bloom on their backs and wings, which so soon disappears in museum specimens.

Swallow-tailed kites. Painting by Walter Weber, courtesy of the estate of Walter Weber.

> I shall never forget the loving reverence with which the noted
> bird artist admired his specimen, as he began at once to sketch
> its charms.

One side of my mind continues to wonder how these killings could
take place so casually. You can easily detect the sense of guilt by people who should have known better, even in those days.

Another noble raptor, the red-shouldered hawk, poses for us on a
dead tree stub out in the open, clearly showing his red shoulders. I
used to see red-shouldered hawks every spring back home in Dover,
New Hampshire, along the Cocheco River, but not for the last fifty
years. That is one of the benefits of our parks, the birds and animals
have acquired a certain amount of freedom from fear. Highlands Hammock State Park has a noble history. It was donated to the state by a
group of enlightened conservationists even before the state park system was established officially, way back in 1931, years before such a
thing became more popular. The contribution was spurred especially
by the Roebling family, who later became well known for their gen-
erosity in preserving other state gems, such as the Archbold Biological
Station nearby. Yes, Virginia, there are Santa Clauses out there. One
hopes that future generations will produce equal numbers of environmental activists and benefactors who will continue to make a difference in saving the remaining bits of wilderness in the great state of
Florida. It's actually a wonder that anything is left after all the up-
heaval and overpopulation that took place in the twentieth century.

In March and April 1955, near this same Sebring-Okeechobee area,
I made one of my more memorable solo trips, one that lasted for five
weeks. I met and went birding with the late Alexander Sprunt Jr. of
National Audubon Society fame. Sprunt was also the author of several
good books, including *South Carolina Bird Life* (Sprunt and Chamberlain 1949) and the rewrite of Arthur Howell's *Florida Bird Life*
(Sprunt 1954). One of my favorites is *The Warblers of North America*
(Griscom and Sprunt 1957), coedited with Ludlow Griscom, the dean
of New England birding in the 1940s and 1950s.

Impressionable as I was on that trip, I have never met a person,
before or since, who knew so much about birds and was such a per-
sonable live wire. I think one of the most impressive things of the five
days afield was Sprunt's skill at seeing the birds while driving, con-

stantly looking back and forth and around, in between stealing glances of the road. It may be of interest to list the birds (as the names were known at that time) we saw on 29–30 March around portions of Okeechobee, Glades, and Highland Counties: pied-billed grebe, double-crested cormorant, anhinga, great blue heron, American egret, snowy egret, cattle egret, tricolored heron, little blue heron, glossy ibis, white ibis, mottled duck, gadwall, baldpate, pintail, green-winged teal, blue-winged teal, shoveler, ring-necked duck, lesser scaup duck, turkey vulture, black vulture, red-tailed hawk, red-shouldered hawk, bald eagle, marsh hawk, Audubon's caracara, kestrel, sandhill crane, gallinule, American coot, killdeer, greater yellowlegs, lesser yellow-legs, least sandpiper, dowitcher, black-necked stilt, herring gull, ring-billed gull, Bonaparte's gull, Caspian tern, black skimmer, mourning dove, ground-dove, belted kingfisher, eastern kingbird, phoebe, tree swallow, purple martin, blue jay, crow, fish crow, mockingbird, robin, loggerhead shrike, palm warbler, meadowlark, red-winged blackbird, boat-tailed grackle, purple grackle, towhee, and savannah sparrow, for a grand total of sixty-two species.

There is nothing out of the ordinary in this list—even today. Although the loggerhead shrike is declining drastically further north, it appears to be holding its own in parts of open-country Florida. Audubon's caracara (now crested caracara), although threatened, can still be found in this area, but in smaller numbers than Sprunt and I saw them. One hundred fifty pairs concentrate west and north of Lake Okeechobee on the few surviving prairies. On another day, we saw the burrowing owl, a common resident of the Okeechobee area and throughout most of Florida. Apparently, the owl's numbers are actually increasing because of the continued cutting of trees in the state. According to Pranty (1996), the population is said to vary between 5000 and 10,000 birds in recent years.

A boat trip on Florida Bay and a visit to the Everglades National Park added several specialties: the roseate spoonbill, man-o'-war bird (now called the magnificent frigatebird), flamingo, brown pelican, limpkin, more swallow-tailed kites, reddish egret, Forster's tern, and royal tern. Again, all of these species are still seen here forty-five years later, but in much smaller numbers. Other people on this boat trip were Charlie Brookfield of Audubon Society fame, Ed Rowell, Otto Ger-

A limpkin. Everglades National Park, Dade County, Florida, March 1955.

Roseate spoonbills from the excellent book *The Art of Basil Ede: Wild Birds of America* (1991).

schner, and Mr. and Mrs. Philip Grosch. There is nothing in the bird world more beautiful than the roseate spoonbill, and nobody knows them better than Robert Porter Allen, who spent thirty years with the National Audubon Society as sanctuary director and researcher. In his famous monograph, *The Flame Birds* (1947), Allen described a "never before observed spectacle," more than 100 males and females congregated in one spot:

> I suffered from the feeling that I was an interloper, an intruder. That my presence was a desecration. . . . They won't do anything I grumbled. In this mood the explosion that took place, without warning, was more startling than it might have been earlier. It shook me quite as much as an explosion . . . an eruption of the entire pink flock, a mass ascent, three hundred pairs of pink and carmine wings. The sound was indescribable, overpowering. It was like a blow between the eyes, and I was literally stunned by it. The great flock swept before me in a mad rush of swishing, flashing wings, outstretched necks and heads, rigid legs. In an instant the visible world was filled with a confused, careening mass of pink birds; in another the roar of sound had ceased, the hurtling bodies, the confusion of wings had disappeared. . . . What I had witnessed was indeed the beginning of the Spoonbill's complex reproductive cycle. As a spectacle these up-flights are one of the most thrilling sights in all Nature, a vivid and breath-taking ritual that would be magnificent in any large bird. With the Roseate Spoonbill as the principal, it is a drama of unequaled beauty.

In the 1800s the roseate spoonbill was hunted nearly to extinction for women's hats and other finery. The spoonbill is making a slow recovery, especially since the 1940s, and has extended its breeding range along the entire west coast of Florida, part of the Louisiana coast, and all of the Texas coast—in suitable wetlands near both salt and fresh water. But the increasing depletion of wetlands through urbanization remains the critical factor for the bird's future survival.

And so we come to a crossroads in the great state of Florida. After being carved up and bled dry, the Everglades may finally get a chance to heal. We can only hope it will be saved for its own and posterity's sake.

CHAPTER 10

Bombay Hook and Prime Hook National Wildlife Refuges

T HE SUN is rapidly setting behind me, a thin veil of cirrus transforming the sky from bleakness to brightness in a matter of minutes, fairly demanding the photographer's attention—but not this evening. In front of me, against a darkened gray sky, another part of nature's mural is transfiguring the massive muddy marshland. Colossal flakes of snow on the far horizon change into hundreds of miniature white aircraft stretched in long lines, sweeping slowly, descending gradually, ever closer, wave after wave, finally revealing the shape of snow geese in the glow of the setting sun. Then, presto, the white birds land in the darkening dusk and blanket the black muck. I pick up the first line on the far horizon and follow it until hundreds of wings set to alight in front of us. This scene repeats itself again and again for two hours. There is no control tower, only loud shrill honking from thousands of birds, who perform an annual rite in front of two awestruck human beings. Imagine 25,000 to 50,000 great white birds (and a few blue ones) filling the sky and marsh less than 200 yards in front of us. In another part of these vast marshes, as if they know their own landing rights, smaller flocks of thousands of Canada geese approach and land, but they do not mix with the snows at all.

Each October this spectacular sight takes place on Bombay Hook National Wildlife Refuge's 15,000 acres of tidal marsh and water impoundments, located below Dover, Delaware, on the shores of Delaware Bay. To a lesser extent, the geese also come to Prime Hook National Wildlife Refuge, located south of Bombay, which has only 8800 acres. For most of these geese, these refuges are home for the winter. The sight of watching the geese fly in is unforgettable. Although some people compare it with other extraordinary animal movements, such as the wildebeest in Africa, it reminds me of the gannets on St. Bonaventure Island in the Gaspé of Québec, Canada. Which is the greatest experience? That's a difficult question to answer, but I think my vote would go with the gannets.

Incidentally, the snow and blue geese were long considered separate species. But in the always-changing world of taxonomy, they are now considered to be morphs, that is, alternative color forms of the same species. Although the botanical world is more notorious for such taxonomic shifting, especially with phylogenetics and cladistics assuming far more importance in deciding relationships, the American Ornithologists' Union regularly changes names, too, sometimes back and forth.

As we pry ourselves away from the snow geese spectacle, a 12-mile

Thousands of snow geese coming in on their annual fall migration to Bombay Hook National Wildlife Refuge, Kent County, Delaware, late in the day of 5 October 1994.

drive around the refuge reveals many species of ducks, notably on this day, a few dozen ruddy ducks just below me, which we see rarely in northern New England, their white faces bleached by the lowering sun against the dark shadows of the water. We also see blue-winged and green-winged teals, widgeons, gadwalls, pintails, wood ducks, black ducks, as well as the usual egrets, herons, and shorebirds. It is during May, however, that one sees the refuges' other spectacle: the annual horseshoe crab egg feast, which the shorebirds (notably red knots, turnstones, and black-bellied plovers) attend to in a feeding frenzy by the thousands. This stop is crucial in preparation for their long flight to the Arctic breeding grounds.

At Prime Hook, a boat is the preferred method of transport. Unfortunately, we do not have a boat, so we don't see as many ducks as we might have otherwise. Nevertheless, the prime sight for me is the flock of two dozen blue-winged teals. Their trademark shoulder patches, the bright blue epaulets, flash with each twist and turn of the flock, which moves in a tight formation low over the water. Although not as spectacular as the snow geese in terms of sheer numbers, the wheeling

Ruddy ducks in waning daylight. Bombay Hook National Wildlife Refuge, Kent County, Delaware, 5 October 1994.

A great egret and its reflection. Bombay Hook National Wildlife Refuge, Kent County, Delaware, 5 October 1994.

flight of one of our smallest ducks—akin to flocking sandpipers—is spectacular for its precision; how the individuals in the flock maintain their positions during the split-second turns with nary a bump or accident still befuddles the experts. Audubon described it best: "When flying in flocks in clear sunny weather, the blue of their wings glistens like polished steel, so as to give them the most lively appearance, and while they are wheeling over the places in which they intend to alight, their wings being alternately thrown into the shade and exposed to the bright light, the glowing and varied luster thus produced, at whatever distance they may be, draws your eyes involuntarily toward them." In our case, it is a cloudy day, so instead of alternating as polished steel, the large blue shoulder patches are striking at every turn of the flock, enhanced by the ducks remarkable aerial acrobatics. The blue-winged teal is more wary than many ducks; it takes to the air at the slightest perceived disturbance, passing and repassing for many seconds over the water before finally feeling safe enough to alight again. Watching the blue-winged teal is easily one of the more memorable birding displays. The green-winged teal, in contrast, has a much smaller iridescent green wing patch at the rear of the wing (on the secondaries, or speculum, rather than on the forewing, as in the blue-winged). Consequently, in flight the green-winged does not have the pizzazz or flamboyant elegance of the blue-winged teal.

Despite their close relationship, the green-winged teal is much hardier than the blue-winged, reaching its more northern breeding grounds earlier and remaining further north in the winter. The blue-winged teal is known to fly as far south as Argentina in the winter, one of only about a dozen non-sandpiper North American nesters who do; one bird shot in Peru and banded in Saskatchewan, Canada, had covered 7000 miles. Most, however, stick around northern South America and Central America. A marvel of flight expertise, the speed of the teals sometimes has been overrated; apparently, 45 miles per hour is the normal maximum, rather than the 150 miles per hour some previously thought, making the blue-winged, along with the green-winged teal, still one of the fastest birds in flight. The prize, however, belongs to the peregrine falcon, which has been clocked at more than 150 miles per hour while diving in pursuit of prey, although peregrines move only in the range of 40 miles per hour under normal flight patterns. The teals have few enemies, except for raptors and animals who rob their nests and, perhaps the most harmful, the human hunter and wetlands destroyer.

Also at Prime Hook, which is, in general, better than Bombay Hook for ducks, we see the most shovelers I've seen anywhere—two dozen to be exact—and as many as 100,000 tree swallows on their way to South America. Nearby, in the Little Creek Wildlife Management Area, about 500 avocets rest, unfortunately at too great a distance to enjoy, but still a first for most of us. Several taller-than-usual cardinal flower

A blue-winged teal. Painting by Basil Ede, courtesy of Basil Ede and the Gulf States Paper Corporation.

plants (*Lobelia cardinalis*) caught my eye in the ditch on the way in and I have to stop and measure one of them—an amazing 8 feet.

This trip is sponsored by the Audubon Society of New Hampshire. Our leader is Bob Quinn, a freelancer long associated with the society in different capacities. The original destination is Cape May, New Jersey, where we witness the annual hawk flight. On this day in early October, we see several dozen sharp-shinned hawks, Cooper's hawks, and turkey vultures; more than a dozen red-tailed hawks and kestrels; a half dozen or more harriers; and two or three osprey. Despite the northwesterly breeze, the totals are not as good as most days at old Cape May, we learn. Due to the earlier-than-normal cool weather, the main warbler flights occurred before we arrived, so we settle for a yellow-throated, a black-throated blue, a redstart, six yellow-rumped, and several western palm warblers. Twenty-five American and one Eurasian widgeon rest on the pond off the Cape May Point State Park parking lot. Twenty-four Forster's terns and the dominant laughing gulls make their presence felt. Fifty to a hundred blue jays are obviously preparing to fly further south, as are a couple dozen flickers, hundreds of tree swallows, a singing Carolina wren, and an immature dickcissel visiting from the West. We encounter fish crows—downtown, no less— their nasal *car* notes drawing our attention after eating lunch. We see sixty species of birds, including all the so-called paddle ducks and all the herons and egrets, except for the reddish egret and glossy ibis, the latter now a common bird in spring in the Scarborough Marshes below Portland, Maine.

The vegetation, as always, is an important part of the day at Higbee Beach: persimmon, post oak, southern red oak, black walnut, American holly, red cedar, bayberry, beach plum, and winged sumac, the latter four also dominant at Parker River National Wildlife Refuge back home in New Hampshire. The pretty little sea pink (*Sabatia stellaris*) still carries some blooms at this late date, and we come across the remarkable saltwort (*Salsola*), a rather unusual, very thorny plant with prolific bright red bracts that look like many red flowers.

We spend two days at Cape May, take the ferry across Delaware Bay to the town of Lewes, Delaware, and drive northward to Bombay Hook and Prime Hook. Then the long ride back to New Jersey, by land this time, up and around Wilmington, Delaware, and back down again to

Wildwood Crest, New Jersey. We arrive well after midnight, too long a ride for what remains to be seen. The next day, we spend time in our final refuge, the Brigantine-Forsythe on the coast north of Atlantic City, which encompasses 36,000 acres of coastal marshland. The most noteworthy experience, from my perspective, occurred on a very warm day as we joined up with the leisurely flight of monarch butterflies and yellow-rumped warblers on the beach dunes. The birds respond to the warmth with droopy wings, displaying their yellow rump badges even more noticeably than usual. For more than an hour, this movement continues uninterrupted, just as it probably does every year. We also see a small flight of the brant for which this refuge is noted; some 80,000 (20 percent of the entire Atlantic population) may winter here. Brants nest further north along the Arctic coasts than most waterfowl, where nesting success is unpredictable. Also unpredictable is their main source of nourishment, the eelgrass, the lack of which almost forced the brant into extinction in the 1930s. Overall, however, this final stop proves the least enjoyable of the entire trip. Perhaps it is because we do not have the time to stop in the nearby New Jersey Pine Barrens to catch the famous Pine Barrens gentian blooming at this same time. I am traveling with my birding companions, however, so plants are not one of the targets on this journey. I have yet to see it.

CHAPTER 11

Gannets on the Gaspé in Québec

MY MOTHER and father spent a week on vacation on the Gaspé in Québec when I was in grade school. As is the wont of a young guy, thoughts of someday repeating the experience remained in my mind for those uncounted following years. By the time it became possible, of course, the object had changed from one of leisurely scenery to gannets on a rock, specifically the St. Bonaventure Island rocks, 2 miles offshore from the village of Percé on the Gaspé.

On everyone's list of ten best North American birding destinations, Percé is a tourist attraction for other reasons, too. Percé Rock is the focus of much attention, as is Forillon National Park, a few miles up the coast from the village of Percé. When visiting, you should take the boat ride that completely circles the nearly round, 2-mile-wide, 300-foot-high rock. That way you see the thousands of seabirds clinging to the sheer seaward-facing cliffs, especially if your captain steers as close as he can without risking life or limb. The dominant gannets occupy the tableland on the very edge of the top of the cliffs exclusively, without any encroachment from the other species, which cling precariously just below them on the eastern face of the steep cliffs. Here there is a diversity of razorbills, common murres, black guillemots, Atlantic puffins, and especially the black-legged kittiwake, a gull about the size of a ring-billed (17 inches) with black legs, feet, and wing-tips and a solid yellow bill. The eastern cliff face also holds many younger gannets; apparently, the older birds claim the top of the rock for themselves. John James Audubon described the scene on 14 June 1833: "After awhile I could distinctly see its top from the deck, and thought that it was still covered with snow several feet deep . . . I imagined that the atmosphere around was filled with flakes . . . the pilot smiled at my simplicity and assured me that nothing was in sight but the gannets."

My wife, Susan, comes with me on one boat trip, but remains in Percé the other two times. Three trips are about right when doing both birding and botanizing. And today, the birds are the focus of 99 percent of the tourists. We hike the 1.5-mile trail up a slight rise followed by a gradual descent to the open cliffs on the east side of the island, where all the action is. Anticipation builds, and nothing else can really distract the birder—even orchids—on this first journey, believe me. All is quiet on the wooded pathway until I begin to hear the birds at some distance—remember we are talking about some 50,000 large birds. I know I am close, however, when the smell reaches my nostrils.

The woods stop, the sky reappears, and continuously there are

A gannet colony on St. Bonaventure Island. The Gaspé, Québec, 3 July 1990.

hundreds of white birds in the air. As Roger Tory Peterson said, "The size and whiteness of the gannets give them a visual impact lacking in lesser fowl." But the drama really rests on the ground in front of me— right and left as far as the eye can see. On this narrow shelf sit tens of thousands of gannets, twice the size of seagulls, performing their annual rite of summer, the raising of a single chick. Unfolding in front of me is one of the greatest shows on Earth: an endless ritual of milling, strutting, necking, billing, feeding, and rearranging nesting material, all under a constant din of grunts and cries, a scene of organized and good-natured mayhem. The big birds are so crowded that every foot of ground is utilized right up to the single rail fence, allowing for enjoyment of every detail. (This fence was erected by the Provincial Government of Québec in 1972 to provide separation between the birds and onlookers and photographers doing their thing.) While this commotion takes place, there is a nonstop coming and going of birds, both of which are accomplished with no grace whatsoever. The landings consist of a flump and flop like a disabled aircraft, and the takeoffs require much effort and labor, as you can well imagine, considering

Head and bill profile of a gannet on St. Bonaventure Island. Hand-held extreme close-up taken with a 100-mm macro lens. The Gaspé, Québec, 3 July 1990.

the wall-to-wall nature of the gannetry and the fact that these cigar-shaped birds are 3 feet in length with 6-foot wingspans.

Following almost ninety days of unending attention, the young bird is on its own, first struggling to the edge of the cliff, in a series of flops and wobbles, then jumping off, innately expecting to reach the formidable ocean waters 300 feet below. If it does not clear the rocks, however, the young bird becomes fair game for the predators. But that is only the beginning: After reaching the cold, choppy ocean, the young gannet swims out to sea, unable to fly or dive for another week or two. It requires another three to five years before it, too, can begin to raise young, paired for life, returning to the same rock year after year. Gannets spend winters at sea along the Atlantic Coast from Cape Cod to the Gulf of Mexico, where they can be seen with binoculars from certain vantage points along the shore or from pelagic boats. Gannets regularly dive and splash from heights of 100 feet and more. Their skulls and necks are reinforced and cushioned with air cells to take such devastating blows.

The gannet has recovered from its near extinction of the late 1800s and early 1900s, when fishermen clubbed the chicks for bait. Audubon also depicted that scene: "At sight of these unwelcome intruders, the affrighted birds rise on wing with a noise like thunder, and fly off in such a hurried and confused manner as to impede each other's progress, by which thousands are forced downwards and accumulate into a bank many feet high; the men beating and killing them with their clubs until fatigued, or satisfied with the number they have slain." Current obstacles facing gannets include entanglement in commercial fishermen's gill nets, increasingly frequent oil spills, and competition with the fishing industry for depleted stocks of herring and mackerel. If an individual can avoid these things, however, a gannet may live for twenty years or more, continuing to provide sightseers with picturesque snowstorms in the middle of July on all six remaining gannetries in the North Atlantic. Otherwise the gannet will join the great auk in the great beyond of extinction.

Next to the gannets, the black guillemots are my chief interest on the island. These birds are pitch black, except for a large white wing patch and bright carmine legs and feet. The most extraordinary thing, though, is the equally bright red that lines the inside of the mouth, a remarkable color combination. The guillemots are nesting alone on the west or landward side of Bonaventure Island, quite close to the dock as a matter of fact, so that I am able to sneak up on them among the rocks and boulders at the base of the much lower cliffs on this side of the island. The black body blends so well with the dark rocks that I don't notice them until they move in and out of the holes among the rocks (while resting, the pigeon-sized birds crouch and hide the red legs).

The guillemot is a common bird that floats on the relatively rough waters on our way back to the mainland, until the boat sends them flying low over the water ahead or to the side of us, swinging around in

Black guillemots on St. Bonaventure Island. The Gaspé, Québec, 6 July 1990.

a curve to splash down behind the boat, displaying their full beauty just inches above the water. The monogamous sea pigeon, as the guillemot is known, is a specialist in this environment. It feeds mostly inshore and raises two chicks on a diet predominantly composed of fish, which it can pursue underwater with short but muscular open wings. Like the gannet, the guillemot is pelagic (spending life on and over the ocean) in winter, but unlike the gannet, it remains close to its breeding grounds year-round. Guillemots change color in winter, becoming almost entirely white except for the black wing primaries and black mottling on the back.

The guillemot is a member of the alcid family, whereas the gannet is a booby. Alcids are the ecological counterparts of the penguins of the Antarctic, but these birds are as far apart in their evolution as in their distribution. Even though one of the earliest victims of human-caused extinction, the great auk, was given a scientific name that means penguin (*Pinguinus*), it and all other alcids are entirely different taxonomically from the Southern Hemisphere's true penguins. Standing more than 2 feet tall, the great auk suffered the same fate as most alcids in the far north during their breeding season—even more so because it was flightless: killed relentlessly for food, bait, and feathers for pillows and mattresses. From a population believed to be in the millions, it took fewer than sixty years (1785–1844) to kill them all. Now, of course, alcids are protected from shooting and clubbing, but not from the scourges of gill nets, oil spills, and overfishing.

Our four-day visit to Percé and St. Bonaventure Island did not allow enough time for much land bird exploring, which I regret. In addition, one of the major trails, and the best for birding, was closed for repairs. Although we saw none of the island's nesting warblers, we did see several finches: purple finch, pine siskin, and the handsome evening grosbeak. Time is important for appreciating the scenic qualities of Percé Rock, which is accessible to foot traffic at low tide (you must keep your wits about you on the tides). I preferred the effects of the early sunrise on the rock, waking up with the sun at four o'clock in the morning to photograph the sequence of lighting from our motel front porch, an almost two-hour stretch.

Although the birding is wonderful in Percé, do not expect similar delights for your palate. Our visit confirmed what George Harrison documented in his book *Roger Tory Peterson's Dozen Birding Hot Spots* (1976): seafood and fish dinners are in short supply throughout the Maritimes. I might also add that a working knowledge of French is a great asset while traveling in Québec. In our experience, our French neighbors made few attempts to understand our English throughout the trip. In all fairness, though, we Americans do little or nothing to learn French for the sake of making their time more pleasant while visiting us in the States.

CHAPTER 12

Nesting in Newfoundland

THE SUMMER of 1997 finds me in two extreme corners of North America. On 18 July, in Hawke's Bay on the northern peninsula of Newfoundland, I watch a busy male Wilson's warbler nesting. Exactly one month later, in Tucson, Arizona, I see a male Wilson's warbler in migration. This black-capped warbler breeds from Newfoundland westward across most of Canada all the way to Alaska, where it is common throughout, except for the extreme northern strip. This little warbler, one of the smallest at 4.5 inches, is apparently much more common in the West, which probably explains its early appearance in Tucson. The Wilson's warbler also has a tremendous north–south nesting range (along with the yellow, yellow-rumped, and orange-crowned warblers), stretching from Alaska to the mountains of northern New Mexico.

The Wilson's is one of only five warblers that lay claim to the northernmost nesting grounds and, in a family of about fifty North American species, the only warblers that range from Newfoundland and Labrador in the east to Alaska in the west. The other four species are the blackpoll, yellow, northern waterthrush, and the yellow-rumped. Fourteen warbler species nest in Newfoundland. Compare this with New Hampshire's twenty species and West Virginia's twenty-six, the highest total for any state. Mount Desert (pronounced like "dessert") in the Acadia National Park on the Maine coast, however, rightfully lays claim to the title of "warbler capital of the United States," with a total of twenty-one species of nesting warblers on just that one island. In Newfoundland, the most abundant warblers are the blackpoll and Wilson's, followed by the yellow and northern waterthrush.

The blackpoll and yellow-rumped warblers also nest above 3000 feet in the red spruce–balsam fir forests on the upper slopes of Mount Washington and the higher White Mountains of New Hampshire, where they are the most abundant breeding warblers. These northerners are able to adapt to the cold and wind better than other warblers due to thicker semiplumes and down plumules close to the skin,

A pair of Wilson's warblers. Painting from the early 1900s by Louis Agassiz Fuertes.

which provide more insulation. It is also claimed that their larger size and slower movements help to conserve energy at these higher and colder elevations. The most amazing thing to me, however, is their nearly 5000-mile migration from here to South America and back, which includes a flight farther out to sea than any other warbler. The flight lasts more than sixty hours—nonstop!

Newfoundland's more than 200 species of birds occupy the fifteenth largest island in the world (about the size of Pennsylvania) and the most easterly point of North America. The island's largest city is St. John's, situated on the east coast and located almost halfway between Ireland and New York City: 1650 miles and 1250 miles, respectively. The climate is surprisingly mild, ranging from 50 to 80°F in the summer months and to the teens and twenties in the winter. Temperatures seldom go below 0°F, and then to about −10 or −15°F, with the climate being modified by the ocean. (But don't tell this to the islanders during a blizzard.) In Tucson, a month later, it is 100°F under a blistering desert sun, where a lethargic Wilson's warbler seeks shelter of a different kind—shade. What flexibility in this little black-capped warbler!

A blackpoll warbler on a juniper. Photograph by Dan Sudia.

As a great fan of warblers, I am excited about my first visit to the northern breeding grounds of several species that are only migrants further south. On 15 July 1997, a group of eleven orchid enthusiasts are heading north on the only surfaced highway in northwestern Newfoundland, the celebrated northern peninsula. It rained all last night, but today is mostly cloudy with gusty gale-force winds reaching 70 knots. A pit stop at St. Anthony's airport a few miles south of Cape Norman, the northernmost point on the island of Newfoundland, verifies the wind speed when I climb the stairs to the flight controllers' room. I also learn that this kind of gale surprisingly does not ground the jets or helicopters.

Once back on the road to Cape Norman, we spot the Long Range Mountains, which break the monotony of an extraordinarily flat gray landscape. As we walk in the mountains, which run along the spine of the peninsula, I notice that the ground is pockmarked with clumps of yellow spotted lady's-slippers (*Cypripedium yatabeanum*), frog orchids (*Coeloglossum viride* var. *virescens*), tall leafy green orchids, and the rare Newfoundland orchid (*Pseudorchis straminea*). Bracing ourselves against the wind in 40°F temperatures, we try to photograph some of the ten icebergs floating in the Atlantic Ocean. It is impossible to do much with the many American pipits and horned larks we accidentally send into flight. Most of the orchids, however, grow in niches among the cracked limestone pavement, partially protected from the unrelenting onslaught of the gale, thus allowing us a certain number of photographs.

Later this same day we are back in our motel in Plum Point, Newfoundland, a few miles south of the ferry to Labrador at the south end of the Strait of Belle Isle. Miraculously, the sun is out, the gale is gone. "What do you say, let's take a walk, it's such a beautiful evening?" Anne Wagner from Rhode Island, Ted Watt from New York, and myself take a leisurely stroll along an inlet of the Gulf of St. Lawrence behind the motel. The birds join us in taking advantage of the balmy evening. In less than an hour, we pish and squeak up blackpoll and yellow-rumped warblers, as well as song and savannah sparrows. The warblers observe us nervously from the tops of balsam firs with the usual assortment of *chip* and *check* calls. They hesitate to carry the food hanging from their bills to nearby nestlings while humans watch. Instead of the typical hyperactive movements in migration, tonight it is a real treat to have several seconds of unobstructed viewing while the warblers decide whether to make the final move to their nest. What handsome birds they are in the late, low angled, but still intense sunlight. Yet, in just a few short weeks both male warblers will assume the olive green streaks of the drab females. What a splendid oasis and pleasant interval after a long day of driving through endless flat gray.

A word about squeaking: Some birders believe in it, others do not. In my experience it depends on the bird(s) you are trying to see and the circumstances. It is more successful when birds are feeding their young. Squeaking is produced simply by kissing the back of your hand. Pishing is a variation that involves making a *pish* sound, like the one you used to make in grade school to get the attention of the kid in front of you.

Watching these extreme northern warblers on their home territory for the first time conjures a special feeling that is hard to put into words. Seeing them passing through on migration twice each year is

A yellow-rumped warbler. Photograph by Dan Sudia.

one thing, but this is different—it completes the circle, so to speak. I now have a sense of the journey the warblers make (albeit by way of car and ferry) to these northernmost nesting grounds. Am I being sentimental? I don't think so. Bird migration, especially warbler migration, "vivifies what may be the most compelling drama of the natural world," as Scott Weidensaul said in *Living on the Wind* (1999).

Song, savannah, and white-throated sparrows join in with their call notes. Six of the fourteen species of warblers that nest in Newfoundland are noted on this trip without really trying, including several yellows and singing male Wilson's and northern waterthrushes along alder-willow thickets and various water courses. On the west coast and southern end of the northern peninsula, in addition to commonplace robins, I see a male swamp sparrow feeding young, a couple of fox sparrows, and a single yellow-bellied flycatcher.

In the Rocky Harbor and Gros Morne National Park region, at the base of the northern peninsula, while others play with more green orchids in the ditches, I enjoy a group of four pine grosbeaks (one male) eating the seeds from the large heads of dandelion-like yellow salsify (*Tragopogon dubius*), a flock of six pine siskins, and a perfect view of another northern waterthrush that has flown up from the ground to pose in a nearby shrub. Where's my camera when I need it?

At the Watts Point Ecological Reserve, just south of northernmost Cape Norman, I am amazed by the sound of common loons yodeling from the vast waters of the Gulf of St. Lawrence, shrouded unseen in fog nearly as thick as pea soup on this particularly dreary, drizzly day. The more familiar sounds of the black-backed gulls accompany those of the loon. The herring gull and the plentiful black-backs are the only two common summer gulls in Newfoundland.

Speaking of plentiful, huge moose are all over the place, at least along Provincial Route 430. The moose is the largest and most powerful deer in the world. We see several during the two weeks up and down the west coast, including one burly bull we suddenly came upon at a hazardous corner, apparently killed by a vehicle that could not see it in time to avoid a collision moments before. Slowing down, we watch the giant animal being loaded onto a truck in the opposite lane. A cow, perhaps the bull's mate, trots alongside us on the shores of the scenic East Arm of Bonne Bay, wondering what is going on.

It is rather difficult to comprehend that the moose is an introduced mammal here in Newfoundland—it seems such a perfect fit—but the natural range extends from Nova Scotia to Alaska across the north country. Unable to swim the gap from the mainland, the moose got assistance from humans and has flourished here ever since. Averaging more than 7 feet high at the shoulders and weighing almost 2000 pounds, the male moose is the largest antlered mammal that has *ever* lived on our planet. The broad-bladed antlers are nearly 7 feet across from corner to corner. Occasionally, these monarchs will lock in combat to the point of no return, death, both unable to extricate themselves from the locked horns.

We took the ferry from North Sydney, Nova Scotia, to Port Aux Basques on the extreme southwestern corner of Newfoundland, about a five-hour ride, after two and a half days of driving. The trip would

Great black-backed gulls. Newburyport, Massachusetts, 7 March 1997.

have been easier and quicker if we had flown into St. John's, rented a car, and made the several-hundred-mile, five-hour drive to the west coast. In my case, however, I had excellent company in Anne Wagner and Ted Watt. The three of us carried on a literally nonstop conversation for three days, the subject matter ranging all the way from a personal philosophy of life to family issues, people, politics, and orchids. Quite a menu. More importantly, talking kept us awake, especially the driver of the van, Ted, whom we could not relieve because the rental insurance was under his name only.

For a long time, the best bird book on the island has been Harold Peters and Thomas Burleigh's *Birds of Newfoundland* (1951), with all the paintings and drawings done by Roger Tory Peterson. Unfortunately, the book is now difficult to find on the used-book market and is getting expensive.

CHAPTER 13

Ducks Unlimited

F IFTY YEARS later I still vividly remember an early experience with my favorite waterfowl, the hooded merganser. An early journal entry, dated 29 March 1947, records the events of a late afternoon on the Cocheco River in Dover, New Hampshire:

The two hooded mergansers, a male and female glided lightly across the momentarily sun-splashed waters, diagonally from the right bank of the river down to the tip of the small island separating the first channel from the second, where the water was shaded, dark, and tranquil. Having walked this river so many times, I figured that if I went inland a bit, and came back down from upriver, I would have a better chance. The plan worked. But I had to crawl on my hands and knees the last several yards, taking advantage of their dives. At last the hairy-heads glided into perfect view, barely rippling the calm, dark water, the gorgeous male, his striking crest contracted, cocking his head to the right and then to the left in the most graceful manner imaginable. His crest was expanded previously but lowered just as the trunk of a small tree blocked my vision for an instant. Here they were now in perfect view within 50 feet, the light perfect and the background of dark water complementing the picture. What a thrill. Then the male dives and comes up floating buoyantly—like a cock stopper—his back dripping with sparkling water particles. Now the female goes under like a flash and comes up, the sun sifting through her bushy crest. I was able to time their dives: 7, 11, 12, and 12 for the male, and 7 seconds for the female. I was extremely lucky in seeing the hooded mergansers today, for I had been watching some American mergansers and goldeneyes for a long while before any of the hooded made an appearance. During this time it had started to rain and then turned to snow. It was light at first but continued to increase slowly. It was a splendid scene. The snow falling increasingly heavier made the picture all the more memorable. Then they started floating downstream out near the margin of the rapids. After another few minutes of swimming, something frightened them from downstream—or they just decided to fly further upstream. Straight at me, still on the ground. I got a wonderful view as they whistled past directly in front of me— the whistle of their wings very clear; they disappeared around the bend. The snow was falling even harder now as I knelt in thrilled contemplation, in no hurry to leave after three hours of observation.

A pair of hooded mergansers. Painting by Basil Ede, courtesy of Basil Ede and the Gulf States Paper Corporation.

Since those years, I have had many more encounters with the almost too good-looking hooded merganser along the same Cocheco and several other rivers and ponds in Strafford County, New Hampshire. The species is essentially a freshwater duck—unlike the red-breasted merganser—migrating in late autumn only as far as it has to, keeping ahead of the icing of the rivers and ponds, with most birds ending up in the southern states. Its two cousins, the common (formerly the American) and red-breasted mergansers, do not require fresh water in the winter. Thus, these two species remain farther north, either on large tidal rivers, where the common merganser is often seen with its shining black, white, and red, or on the ocean, where the shaggy crested red-breast keeps company with eiders, oldsquaws, scoters and, at a distance, the loons.

The hooded and common mergansers nest in tree cavities. The hooded is indigenous to North America, nesting primarily around the Great Lakes, southern Québec, and southern Ontario. The common, however, nests across the central part of Canada from Newfoundland to the Yukon, while wintering throughout the United States. The red-breasted merganser does not nest in cavities, preferring the solid ground cover. It also has a circumpolar breeding range that extends further north—across extreme northern Canada into the tundra. According to annual Audubon Christmas Bird Counts and surveys by the Fish and Wildlife Services of Canada and the United States, the common merganser is far and away the most common merganser: Estimates show the common at 650,000, the red-breasted 250,000, and the hooded at 75,000.

The common merganser is certainly one of the most handsome of all our ducks. Its size, profile, and gleaming white sides are diagnostic from some distance. Of all the descriptions in the literature, I place Ned Dearborn's (1903) among the best: "The adult male is very conspicuous with his predominating white plumage, particularly when he is illuminated by sunshine. In the hand, he shows a beautiful combination of colors. His head is dark glossy, iridescent green, the shoulders are black, other parts white, except the abdomen which has a salmon tinge. The bill, feet and legs are vermilion. As one takes such a creature from the water, he cannot help feeling that he has come into the possession of one of earth's rarer beauties." The male common merganser is proud of that breast, especially in courting season, when he lifts himself out of the water to display the pink wash that glows in the sunlight.

When our kids were growing up, I collected U.S. postage stamps, but that hobby ended as soon as they entered high school and had better things to do—a rather typical scenario in most families. I have, however, continued to collect federal duck stamps (or migratory bird hunting stamps, as they are officially known), both signed and mint stamps. Of course, I have many gaps in the collection, especially in the early years where prices scare you out of the market for good. The stamp program has also resulted in a series of limited-edition prints, which have carved out a lucrative (albeit expensive) market of their own. Also, there are two particularly beautiful oversized books on the subject of duck stamps: *Duck Stamps and Prints: The Complete Federal and State Editions* (1988) with an introduction by Joe McCaddin and *Duck Stamps: Art in the Service of Conservation* (1989) by Scott Weidensaul.

The federal duck stamp appeared on the scene in 1934, the same year Roger Tory Peterson's revolutionary field guide to birds hit the bookstores, and both have continued to do extremely well ever since. The early stamps were done in black and white or some other monochrome, but beginning in 1970 (Ross's goose) the stamps were produced in full-color lithography. Understandably, the advent of color stimulated a big surge in sales, both in stamps and prints. As of 1990 the most prolific winner of the annual contest was the waterfowl painter Maynard Reece, with Edward J. Bierly in second place. All duck hunters must purchase these migratory duck hunting stamps and display the signed permits (hence the reason for collecting used, or signed, stamps, similar to the collection of used postage stamps). Mint or unused stamps are more valuable than the used, of course.

In 1971 California issued the first state duck stamp, and Iowa followed in 1972. Maryland and Massachusetts began issuing stamps in 1974. By 1976 nine states were in the duck stamp business, and today all fifty states participate in the program. The first of state duck stamps are the most valuable; historically, sales eventually level off in succeeding state stamp sales. As of 1990 Robert Steiner was the leading artist on state stamps, with twelve to his credit, and the aforementioned Maynard Reece came in at seven.

The hooded merganser is so handsome that federal and state programs regularly feature its good looks on hunting stamps. Two federal stamps were issued in 1968 and 1978; the state programs have featured six representations (as of 1990), with the 1986 New Hampshire depiction easily the best of the lot so far. In terms of contest winners, it is not surprising that the most common waterfowl are also the most popular state stamp subjects. The Canada goose leads the parade with thirty-five stamps (as of 1987). The most popular duck for hunting and eating, the mallard, has been rendered thirty-three times, while arguably the most beautiful, the wood duck, comes in third with thirty-two stamps. The pintail and canvasback follow with twenty-eight and twenty-four, respectively. Then it is a free-fall to the green-winged teal at thirteen. Surprisingly, two of the most beautiful North American ducks, the harlequin and common merganser, received nary a single portrait honor—probably because the harlequin is uncommon and

A flock of mallards in a snowstorm. Cocheco River, Dover, New Hampshire, 14 March 1997.

thus seldom seen and the mergansers, in general, are considered to taste too fishy to be much hunted.

In terms of benefits of the program to the ducks themselves, consider these statistics: Between 1934 and 1990, the federal program had sold more than 100 million stamps, allowing the purchase of more than 50 million acres of wetland habitat, with easements protecting an additional 2 million acres. Through the sales of their prints, the artists became instant millionaires in the 1980s and 1990s, attesting to the great popularity of these little pieces of colored paper and their larger facsimiles. The state programs provide an even broader base of clients. No wonder the competition gets keener and keener each year.

It is interesting to compare the two newest field guides: the third edition of the National Geographic Society's *Birds of North America* (1999) and the American Bird Conservancy's *All the Birds of North America* (1997). For instance, the National Geographic guide breaks down the waterfowl family (Anatidae) into nine categories: the swans and geese, whistling-ducks, perching ducks (wood duck), dabbling ducks, pochards (canvasback), eiders, sea ducks, mergansers, and stiff-tailed ducks (ruddy duck). (Years ago, it was pretty much swans, geese, dabbling ducks, and sea ducks.) In *All the Birds*, on the other hand, we have only two categories: goose-sized swimmers and duck-sized swimmers. The former category includes not only the geese and swans but also the cormorants and loons, whereas in the latter category we have all the ducks, plus the grebes and gallinules (coots). I can understand the rationale for including the cormorants with the ducks because to the nonbirder they do look like large ducks, especially in flight. Even beginning birders have made that mistake more than once. I know I've had to take a second look—and not just forty years ago. As for the grebes and gallinules, the device is strictly for aid in identification, obviously, an innovation used throughout that field guide, which takes a bit of getting used to.

Ducks have always been one of my favorite families. Although coastal New Hampshire is certainly not part of a major flyway, we do get a good variety of species that the interior states lack. Although our numbers of most dabbling duck species do not compare to inland areas, the sea ducks help make up for that deficit. Our two best sea ducks are the common eider (about the largest of all North American ducks) and the harlequin duck (arguably the prettiest of all North American ducks, although you will get some strong arguments supporting the wood duck and others where color is not that important in the decision). The common eider and harlequin can be seen along the southern Maine coast from November through April.

The common eider was not always such a common winter sea duck. Apparently, only one pair bred on the coast of Maine in 1905. By the early 1940s more than 2000 pairs were counted; the trend continued most years until 1967 saw more than 20,000 pairs raising families along the Maine coast. The common eider is circumpolar in distribution, extending in winter only as far as Long Island and the islands off Cape Cod, where as many as 500,000 eiders have been counted in the winter.

My best days with the common eider never produced those numbers, of course, but I have seen them up close and personal. On 14 April 1995, I was birding at the mouth of the Scarborough River near the

A flock of harlequin ducks on wintering grounds off the southern Maine coast feeding in shallow rocky margins of high tide along the famous Marginal Way and Bald Head Cliff. Ogunquit, Maine, January 1996.

Scarborough marshes (a fine spot in their own right for migrating waterfowl, egrets, glossy ibis, and shorebirds) in York County, Maine's southernmost county. The conditions were just right for a concentration of eiders in the mouth of the river, that is, the tide was on its way out during the busiest time for migration, mid-April. Some of the more than 5000 eiders flew up the river in short bursts to better position themselves for fishing on the rapidly moving outgoing tide. Other groups took up positions in the shallow water along the sandy beach, merely skimming the surface for easy pickings, in the style of the paddle ducks. I could clearly make out their bills seining below water. Watching this unusual fishing method kept me occupied for over an hour at Pine Point.

The spectacled and Steller's eiders breed strictly in coastal northwestern Alaska and northeastern Siberia and winter near the Aleutians and Bering Sea. The king eider is circumpolar, with most of its winter

A flock of common eiders feeding in the shallow Scarborough River Estuary during the ebb and flow of tides. Pine Point, Maine, 14 April 1995.

range divided between the waters around Newfoundland and the Maritimes in the Northeast and the southeastern Alaska–British Columbia coastlines in the Pacific Northwest.

Between November and April, harlequin ducks winter along the southern Maine coast. (Long Island and Rhode Island represent the southern limit of their winter grounds.) I often spend time at Bald Head Cliff in York, Maine, and the Marginal Way in Ogunquit, Maine. What a place to spend the winter. If you are not familiar with it, the harlequin is an unexpectedly small duck: 17 inches compared to the common eider's 25 inches. The harlequin keeps to the rocky surf at all times, whereas the eiders tend to ebb and flow with the tide, coming in to feed at high tide and loafing around out at sea later, frequently in rafts varying from a few dozen to those in the hundreds and thousands; single and paired birds and small groups are also common. The slate blue, maroon, chestnut, and white harlequins can frequently be spotted tak-

A wonderful scene of an adult male common eider alighting beside a female in the choppy sea. Painting by Basil Ede, courtesy of Basil Ede and the Gulf States Paper Corporation.

ing time out for a nap—always short in duration—on the exposed rocks between the tide levels. I have never seen them on the rocks at high tide or low tide, just as the tide is on its way out; as the rocks begin to reappear, the harlequins swim easily on and off the seaweed-cropped shoulders. Careful scanning of the rocks is necessary because the dark blue body color of the ducks blends with the dark rocks and seaweed. The Maine coast is where I have managed to take the best photographs, by moving in spurts behind the rocks while the ducks are underwater. They dive in unison with no sentry posted above the surface at any given time, so a judicious approach while they are underwater is the best strategy for both observation and pictures.

My best day for the harlequin on the southern coast of Maine was 8 January 1999, when I counted more than fifty, almost evenly split between the Marginal Way at Perkins Cove and Bald Head Cliff near the town line separating Ogunquit and York. These certainly are the easiest places to get the best views of the harlequin. In terms of numbers, however, Isle au Haut, located southeast off the coast of Maine, supposedly harbors the greatest concentration of this duck in the entire western Atlantic (about 150). Of course, seeing the harlequin on the island requires a boat trip in winter conditions.

In the summer, harlequins nest beside streams in Iceland, the southwestern coast of Greenland, and eastern Labrador. The ducks swim to the bottom of the stream and walk like dipper birds, feeding on various insect nymphs and larvae. Winter fare includes barnacles and snails that they scrape off the sides of the rocks. Harlequins usually keep to themselves, in small groups of a half dozen to as many as two dozen. Except when people climb down over the rocks, which sends the ducks out to sea, the birds are always in close among the sharpest rocks and roughest waves, often diving through the middle of the cresting waves. When the sun is shining on these lords and ladies, one can most appreciate the words of Frank Bellrose in his classic *Ducks, Geese and Swans of North America* (1976): "The harlequin duck male is the most bizarrely colored waterfowl, as though a whimsical artist had decorated a deep blue duck with random but precise white-painted markings of various shapes and sizes." The sun makes a great deal of difference—think of a painting in a dimly lit gallery as compared to a well-lit one.

The scoters and oldsquaws are other associates of the eiders and harlequins on the southern Maine coast in winter. Only the white-winged scoter is dependable every day in any numbers. The black and surf scoters are more common in migration than in winter on our northern coast, and they tend to spend their time further out to sea, where strong optics are necessary to see them. The black scoter is the most rare of the three, the smallest, and the only all-black North American duck, if one overlooks its bright orange yellow knob at the base of the bill, a distinguishing character on the water, which accounts for its nicknames of butter-nose and butter-bill. The white wing patch of the larger and heavier white-winged scoter is diagnostic, as is the small white crescent under the white eye. The bill also has knobby protuberances, or swellings, of black at the base, with small amounts of red and yellowish orange at the tip. The surf scoter, intermediate in abundance between the other two, has the most swollen bill of the three, with distinctive white and reddish yellow markings, but the two large white patches on the forehead and the nape are the most distinctive. Female scoters are most easily identified by the company they keep.

The oldsquaw is by far the most entertaining duck, especially as spring approaches. You can hear the bird all winter long, but at revved up speeds in March and April. Musical notes, some expressed as *coween* or *ow-ow-oodle*, carry great distances on a calm day. The loquacious nature of the oldsquaw has spawned more nicknames than just about any other duck: calloo, old Billy, old wife, hound, and south-southerly, to name just a few. Oldsquaws are among the most active in flight, twisting and turning like a flock of sandpipers until plopping into the water with a splash. Unlike any other duck, the male has a long tail (giving rise to such colloquial names as long-tailed duck and old injun) that is easily seen in the wind; the tail is mostly white (or, more accurately, piebald) with black and white patches throughout. Another unique feature of the oldsquaw is that in breeding plumage the male looks more like the female: a transformation into black and brown as if by magic. It is mind-boggling to consider another, more tragic event in the life of this colorful duck: During an eight-week period in spring 1946, for example, 27,000 oldsquaws were caught in the nets of a single Great Lakes fisherman. Despite such slaughter, this bird has recovered fairly well because of the decrease in commercial fishing. But extensive lake freezes also take their toll because old-squaws bond to their wintering grounds.

There is much to see on a ride to the southern Maine coast from late October to late April. A walk along the Marginal Way—with lunch at the Hurricane Restaurant—in tiny Perkins Cove is always exhilarating and usually productive. If you feel more rambunctious, follow the coast to Bald Head Cliff down the road apiece, where we sometimes spend a weekend at the Cliff House. Birders are always welcome on this property, whether or not you stay there. If you do stay, however, the best of both worlds is at your doorstep (considering, of course, that in midwinter you can be subject to bitter cold wind and the occasional snowstorm). It's quite an adventure, though, if you dress properly, not to mention the rewards at the end of the day: a warm fireplace, good food, and even more wave-tossed seabird watching from the comfort of your room overlooking the sheer quartzite cliffs of Bald Head.

CHAPTER 14

The White-headed Woodpecker in California

IN 1956, on perhaps the most extraordinary solo excursion of my life—eleven weeks by automobile to the Pacific Northwest—I tallied the aptly named white-headed woodpecker. I found the bird on the western slopes of the mighty Sierra Nevada in Sequoia National Park, home of the largest living things on the planet—the giant sequoias—as well as incense cedar, ponderosa pine, and the ubiquitous but nonetheless beautiful Steller's jay. Early in the morning, with cooking smoke curling skyward through the shafts of sunlight that find openings in the tall sequoias and sugar pines, North America's largest pine, the 9-inch white-headed woodpecker was the first bird to greet me on a most pleasant morning. I even managed a photograph, but, like other early attempts with an inexpensive fixed-lens camera, the results were expectedly disappointing.

During this trip I spent a weekend with my close friend, Raymond Alie, stationed with his new family at Moses Lake Air Force Base in eastern Washington. Ray and I grew up across the street from each other in Dover, New Hampshire, and have been friends our entire lives, a rarity in this day and age. Because I was unmarried and able to take unpaid time off from work that year, the eleven weeks proved workable. A trip of a lifetime—I visited all our national parks in the Northwest, from the Grand Tetons and Yellowstone to Yosemite and Mount Ranier. My scenic slides, I might add, were generally first rate, capturing much of the majesty and wonder of these priceless national parks and monuments. Other scenic highlights included Glacier National Park and the entire coast of Oregon, much of which, thankfully, even in 1956, was set aside as state parks.

The white-headed is the only North American woodpecker with a white head. The white extends well below to the throat, whereas a large white wing patch shows only in flight. A small red spot on the back of the head of the male can be seen in the proper light and angle, otherwise this bird has an all-black body. The white-headed woodpecker tends to nest low in these giant trees, making it easier to spot even without binoculars. The nesting hole usually ranges from 3 to 15 feet in height. According to Bent (1939), this quietly unassuming woodpecker is so closely attached to pine trees for nesting sites and pine seeds for food that their feathers are almost always smeared with pitch.

Woodpeckers are associated with trees and cavities in trees. They are one of the most distinctive, popular, and easily recognized groups of birds. Unlike most birds, woodpeckers are usually sedentary with little or no seasonal movement, which promotes year-round interest. About twenty-four species represented by five or six genera constitute the Picid family in North America. The downy and hairy woodpeckers are the most widespread, ranging in every state and province from

A white-headed woodpecker. Photograph by Denny Mallory, courtesy of the Cornell Laboratory of Ornithology.

Newfoundland to Alaska and Florida to California. I have seen about half of these woodpecker species.

The crow-sized pileated woodpecker, the amazing cock-of-the-woods, is easily the most exciting and awesome member of the family. The bird is most striking in flight, with its flashing white underwings and bright red crest. The pileated may give us a vicarious sense of what

A male downy woodpecker at our suet feeder. Note the red on his nape. Dover, New Hampshire, 10 February 2000.

A female downy woodpecker (without the red on the nape). Dover, New Hampshire, 10 February 2000.

Adult and juvenile pileated woodpeckers. Photograph by Ted Wilcox, courtesy of the Cornell Laboratory of Ornithology.

it must have been like for early ornithologists to glimpse the magnificent ivory-billed woodpecker, now extinct, in the thickest swamps of the southeastern states during the nineteenth century. Even today people of this region still mistake the pileated for the ivory-billed, for the former remains relatively common in the Southeast. In New Hampshire, I have to work harder to get a good look at this bird, and that look is often merely a flash across the road as I drive, for example, through Franconia Notch in the White Mountains in the northern part of the state. Or a fleeting glimpse while trekking through a swamp or mixed woods, as my father-in-law and I once did many years ago on Nippo Hill in Barrington, New Hampshire. For several miles we tracked

a shy pileated who never allowed a close approach or showed us more than a glimpse as he moved around various tree trunks with soft call notes, maintaining the proverbial step ahead of us the entire three hours.

One day while scanning a tremendous old elm tree beside the headwaters of the Bellamy River in another corner of Barrington, I discovered a pair of pileated woodpeckers nesting in a hole that must have been close to 100 feet high. I spent hours here observing from my car. Unfortunately, this stately elm, in the throes of the nefarious Dutch elm disease, was on its last limbs and succumbed to the chain saw the following year. While hiking through likely haunts, the famous trademark of the pileated is more often seen than the bird itself: several large rectangular (4 × 6 inches and larger) holes excavated from dead or dying tree stubs with

A pileated woodpecker's elliptical workings in a hemlock trunk as it sought carpenter ants and beetles, mostly as winter fare. Barrington, New Hampshire.

the tell-tale wood chip piles on the ground below. These diagnostic excavations are the result of the woodpeckers' search for carpenter ants deep into the heartwood. What is it about these remarkable birds that allows such tremendous pounding to the head? The answer lies in the thick-walled skull, the cushion of space between it and the brain, and the strong muscles in the head and neck—muscles that also propel the tremendous strokes of the bill. Henry David Thoreau, the great nineteenth-century New England naturalist, never saw the pileated woodpecker, but Alexander Wilson and John James Audubon did, many times in Pennsylvania and points south.

The pileated is another example of the pedantry existing among some ornithological taxonomists in terms of vernacular names. As early as 1731 Catesby, perhaps our earliest naturalist, called it the large red-crested woodpecker, while the common folk knew it as the log-cock. A hundred years later, both Wilson and Audubon went along with the establishment's formal scientific name of *pileatus*, and so the die was cast for succeeding generations. It reminds me of a similar situation involving the prothonotary warbler vis-à-vis the golden swamp warbler. Not all that bad, in my opinion.

The red-bellied woodpecker is one of the most common and noisiest (*churr churr churr*) woodpeckers in the eastern half of the country, south of the Great Lakes and New England region, particularly in the Southeast, where I have seen all of my examples of this woodpecker until this past winter. On 10 February 2000, we had a vividly colored male at our suet feeder, an increasingly common sight in southern and central New England in recent years. The eyes are drawn to the electric bright orange to scarlet head and nape. Later you may notice the black and white ladder-back—typical of several other southwestern members of the family—with just a slight wash of red on the tannish lower belly between the legs, which is almost impossible to notice at a distance. Nevertheless, this bit of tint is the source of the common name. Chalk up one more misnomer.

I set up my Canon and 70–300-mm zoom lens on a bean bag cushion against the library window, just 4 feet away from the Parkman crabapple tree stub holding the chicken-wired suet. I sat and waited a full half hour before the red-belly took another chance with the suet, all the while playing hide-and-seek at a safe distance. Perseverance

A red-bellied woodpecker, a rare visitor to our state, at our backyard suet feeder. You can barely see the tinge of scarlet on the belly of this seemingly misnamed woodpecker. Dover, New Hampshire, 10 February 2000.

paid off, as the accompanying shots demonstrate, partly because I earlier lifted the inside windowpane up out of the way, leaving only the outside storm window between the bird and the lens. This produced a clearer picture than two panes of glass, the bane of bird photography from inside the house in wintertime. Seldom have I had the opportunity for two hours of photographing such an animated subject close up. A beautiful adult red squirrel alternated with the red-belly during this two-hour stretch, giving me more exceptionally lucky opportunities to photograph so closely.

It is the little downy woodpecker, however, that is the most familiar and dependable visitor to the suet, day after day, year in and year out. Most observers express a similar sentiment by citing the downy as a model of patient industry and perseverance. The downy never seems to vary in numbers from year to year when I tally my annual New Hampshire Audubon winter feeder census in early February. It is the smallest of all the woodpeckers, nearly 3 inches smaller than its look-

A red-bellied woodpecker works our suet feeder. Dover, New Hampshire, 10 February 2000.

Again, note the red tinge on this red-bellied woodpecker. Dover, New Hampshire, 10 February 2000.

alike, the hairy woodpecker. The downy is much less shy than the hairy, which I find the most difficult bird to photograph at my feeder—the bird flies off at the slightest movement. Many times over the course of a winter, after eating its fill of suet, the downy will sit in place for as much as ten minutes or more—unusual with most birds—relaxed, rested, and perhaps surfeited, even if I am at the window watching. The birds sit like this especially during periods of extreme cold and wind, when our feeding nook is sheltered from the worst of the onslaught.

Each summer the parents introduce their offspring to the dependable food source outside my window. Due to all the hard work of raising a family, the adults are a sorry-looking pair during this relatively short period of time. They remain dirty and bedraggled until the postnuptial (now called prebasic by some authors) molt in late summer, which renews most of the feathers gradually so the bird does not lose the ability to fly at any time. The downy woodpecker is the one we hear most often during the spring drumming season, which follows the sap running. Both sexes drum, and some speculate that drumming corresponds or substitutes for the singing that genuine songbirds perform. Anything that resonates loud enough will do, including gutters, drains, and other metal objects. We hear the drumming almost every spring outside our house. And, of course, during the mating season males do not appreciate other contenders in the wings. This explains the occasional scene of a male pecking away at his own mirror image in a window of our house. One year, a male even chiseled part of the hardened putty holding the windowpane.

For the most detailed information on this and eight other eastern woodpeckers, read Lawrence Kilham's *Woodpeckers of Eastern North America* (1992). In his introduction, Kilham noted an interest in their total behavior: "how they scratched, preened, foraged, bred, interacted with other species, and communicated by means of displays, drumming and vocalizations." Among other things, he discussed one of the oddities I have noticed over the years feeding these birds: their head patterns. Kilham claimed he has never found two downies with the same head pattern. (I cannot say the same.) He diagramed several variations, both in the red spot and the black markings. As a result, Kilham said that he was able to distinguish his study individuals throughout his extensive research on this species. I also have noticed—at the feeder in winter—variation in size of the male's red spot, as well as double red spots (the usual one red area split into two spots).

Another woodpecker is one of my first bird acquaintances, one whom I met in early May 1942. My mother had just exclaimed about a bird in her blooming white apple tree. When I arrived at the window to look, lo and behold, New England's second largest woodpecker, the flicker, lifted into the air at just the right angle, fully displaying its magnificent underwings lined with gold, an eye-opener we had never seen before. Repeat performances in the ensuing years always remind me of that first unforgettable experience, as does picking up a gold-tinted molted wing feather in late summer. The flicker's annual spring wake-up series of *wicker* calls signals the return of spring as much as just about any other sound. Later, the soft courting calls of *yucker-yucker-yucker* direct our attention to the nesting tree. The most opportune time to get a really good look, though, is when the bird is on the ground searching for ants. The flicker is very cautious at these times, and one must be equally so when approaching the window to look. The slightest movement will send it winging up into a tree, the conspicuous white rump flag abruptly disappearing—as does the bird—when it alights in a tree.

The flicker is an adroit anteater. Sometimes in the early autumn, if you are perfectly still—and lucky—you will be treated to a family gathering of flickers foraging together at an anthill in a small clearing in the woods. Back in the days of the Biological Survey in the U.S. Department of Agriculture, whose object was to determine how beneficial or destructive birds were to the economic well-being of our forefathers, Edward Howe Forbush (1925) noted the stomach contents of one flicker as totaling some 5000 ants, with several others in the 3000 range. Between this practice and that of individual and museum collectors, it is surprising to me that there were enough birds to go around in those days. The handsome flicker is perhaps the most widespread and abundant of all our woodpeckers, which probably accounts for all the colloquial or common names it has acquired—an amazing 125 according to Forbush.

My most sensational look at a northern flicker occurred today, 17 March 2000, just a few minutes ago, as I write this chapter. Yesterday broke all records for the warmest 16 March here in southern New Hampshire when it hit 72°F, melting all the snow we received the week before. Last night and this morning, in typical New England fashion, the temperature dropped forty degrees in twelve hours. From 4 to 6 inches of snow fell between midnight and this morning, with wind and temperatures down to 28°F. Not quite one of our famous nor'easters, but close to it. At two o'clock this afternoon, a flock of more than 100 robins—probably the same ones that have been around since January—and many newly arrived bronzed grackles suddenly erupted all over our 'Bobwhite' crabapple, which in chapter 1 I describe as the best late winter emergency food supply for just such days as this one. Anyway, at the same time, a gorgeous male flicker flew in from out of the blue to our suet within arms reach of me at the window. Like an apparition, it shook me up for the few moments it remained, the beauty so overpoweringly close: the red crescent on the nape, the black moustache on the face, and particularly the dipped-in-gold wing primaries and underwing coverts. Just as suddenly, they were all gone with the wind and a tremendous *whisssh*, loud even from inside the house. I knew instantly what caused it, and a quick scan of the trees and shrubs revealed a Cooper's hawk. My chance for the fabulous close-up photograph of the flicker was shattered, but at least it appeared that none of the birds met their end.

The yellow-bellied sapsucker is the only sapsucker found in eastern North America. It has a reputation for drilling holes in trees to drink the sap. In our yard, the European mountain ash was the target. Birches and maples are other favorites, but apparently this sapsucker is not particularly fussy: 246 species of trees have been noted as drilling prospects. Each fall in October the liquid would run from a series of individual holes making up a somewhat square area on the trunk of our mountain ash. Yellow jackets and other insects came in for their share of the liquid refreshment. Ruby-throated hummingbirds are said to also dine at these wells, but I have never seen them. Occasionally, the yellow-bellied sapsucker does serious damage to trees. In the case of the mountain ash, however, this tree is notoriously short-lived and succumbs after ten or fifteen years of providing sumptuous fruit feasts every September and October for the migrating robins and waxwings, among others.

Next to the pileated, my favorite woodpecker is the strikingly colored red-headed woodpecker, a creature of open country, telephone poles, and fence posts along highways east of the Rocky Mountains but south and west of New England. Like the red-bellied, the red-headed has been painfully slow moving into our region. This bird is the only woodpecker with an all-red head—except for a sapsucker restricted to the West Coast of North America that goes by the name of red-breasted sapsucker (its red extending all the way down to include the breast). I always think of our American flag when I see this gorgeous red, white, and dark bluish black beauty in flight. My favorite surroundings are in the Green Swamp's long-leaf pine savannas of North Carolina, where the red-headed woodpecker cavorts with the red-cockaded among the widely spaced, arrow-straight long-leaf pine trees under hot May and June skies. At this time of year and in this part of the coastal plain, my attentions are divided between these active beauties and the equally lovely rosebud orchids (*Cleistes divaricata*) standing at attention as so many alert gazelles on the savannas of Africa. What a juxtaposition of two of the premier sights in this richly endowed ecosystem. The red-headed woodpecker is generally considered the most handsome and most conspicuous of our woodpeckers, its beauty apparently inspiring the great Alexander Wilson to become an ornithologist.

Clear across this great country, in parts of Arizona and New Mexico (with a disjunct population in coastal California), the aptly named acorn woodpecker is one of the most popular and colorful woodpeckers. Pine and oak trees supply the birds' requisite cones and acorns, and soft trees provide places to store them in carefully chiseled holes. Known as the "white-eyed clown of woodpeckers with a harlequin face," this 9-inch woodpecker is communal, nesting and roosting in large family groups of up to a dozen or more. The acorn woodpecker was one of the first birds I became acquainted with on the lower wooded slopes of the Upper Sonoran zone in the famous sky islands of southeastern Arizona (see chapter 4). This and the pretty, pale blue Mexican (Arizona) jays were the most abundant birds in these mountains as well as the most socially conscious and conversational.

Another nut gatherer, Lewis's woodpecker, is dressed in dark green and black except for a gray collar, pinkish breast, and dark red face.

This bird looks like a small version of the American crow, with similar steady wing beats instead of the more usual undulating woodpecker flight pattern. I saw my first Lewis's woodpecker along the dry, monotonous, dusty semi-desert roads of extreme northwestern New Mexico, perched at the top of a telephone pole. We quickly turned around to go back for a closer look at the bird, which is named for Meriwether Lewis, half of the famous team of Lewis and Clark. These explorers made several important new discoveries of plants and animals (birds), but never received their just recognition as two of the greatest early American naturalists, according to some authorities, because of long delays in cataloging and publishing their remarkable collections. Among others, this new woodpecker skin was turned over to Alexander Wilson for identification when Lewis and Clark returned home, whereupon Wilson honored both men with Lewis's woodpecker and Clark's nutcracker. At that time (1808–1814) Wilson was working on his *American Ornithology* and was a great admirer of these patriots, who brought their team home with but a single casualty after twenty-eight months. Another discovery of Lewis and Clark was the pronghorn antelope, my favorite native mammal of the vast open spaces of the far west. For more reading on these two explorers and other famous people commemorated in North American bird names, read the series of absorbing biographies in Barbara and Richard Mearns's *Audubon to Xantus* (1992).

The two species of three-toed woodpeckers have almost exclusively Canadian and boreal ranges in the far north. The three-toed woodpecker was formerly called the Arctic three-toed woodpecker as well as the ladder-backed woodpecker (due to its upperparts being barred with horizontal black and white stripes). The other species is now known as simply the black-backed woodpecker (no longer the ladder-backed woodpecker, at least officially, in the Northeast). The three-toed is rare in eastern North America, but not uncommon in western Canada. Both species prefer burned-over spruce forests and do more bark flaking with their bills, rather than the hole drilling of most other picids, in their search for food. Both of these woodpeckers also nest in extreme northern New Hampshire down to approximately the 3000-foot level in the White Mountains, with the three-toed much more rare than the black-backed. The best time to locate the three-toed and black-backed woodpeckers is in April, when they are the most active. Thanks to the directions of Tudor Richards, a college friend and I located a nesting hole without any difficulty at all. The nest was in a dead stub standing alone in an extensively lumbered clearing, which provided perfect views of the parents coming and going—the birds often allow observers a close approach. Another thing in our favor was the location of the nest hole, which ranges from about 2 to 18 feet in New Hampshire. The nesting locality was in extreme northern New Hampshire in the vicinity of the upper Connecticut Lakes, where the chances of seeing this unusual picid are reasonably good. These species will occasionally move a few miles further south in winter, particularly the black-backed, a movement apparently related more to food than to climate. I have seen the black-backed on at least two occasions in my back-yard in Dover, which is near the coast in southern New Hampshire. Peculiarly, these two species lack any of the red that characterizes every other member of the woodpecker family. The red is replaced by a conspicuous yellow crown, or cap, in the male. Otherwise, they are apparently closely related to the other members of the genus *Picoides* (meaning "resembling a woodpecker").

No matter where birders are, there always seem to be woodpeckers around. You don't have to wait very long to see or hear one, which probably accounts for their great popularity. If people would only leave their dead trees and stubs alone, the natural world would be the richer for it. Most people do not appreciate the tremendous influence woodpeckers have in the lives of so many other birds and animals that depend on their cavities for nesting and roosting sites and escape from the elements.

CHAPTER 15

Hurricane Carol

A s Mark Twain said in a speech in 1876: "I could speak volumes about the inhuman perversity of the New England weather, but I will give but a single specimen." His favorite of all storms was the ice storm because of its "supremest possibility in art or nature of bewildering, intoxicating magnificence." Myself, I favor hurricanes, for other reasons, not the least of which is their connection with some of the greatest birding days as well as their fascinating raw natural force. But the thought of a hurricane fills most people with a sense of foreboding. Since the New England hurricane of 1938, my first experience, when as a boy of ten I was confined to the immediate neighborhood, I had long hoped for an opportunity to experience one firsthand —outdoors in the middle of it.

And so it came to pass on 31 August 1954 when Hurricane Carol pays New Hampshire a visit. My mother, father, siblings, and I are staying at our summer cottage on Great Boars Head in Hampton Beach, New Hampshire. I leave the house at eight-thirty in a rainsquall driven by gale-force winds, on my way to work in Dover, about a half hour inland from Portsmouth, New Hampshire. But there is no way I can sit in my office while such a magnificent display unfolds at the seashore —the pull is simply too irresistible. Back to the coast I go.

I first note small flocks of sanderling-sized birds in the marsh behind Bass Beach, on Route 1A. These are alternately flying above and alighting below in the marshy water holes, which are rapidly filling up with water. They prove to be northern phalaropes seeking shelter, still able to fight back against the increasing gales. At Eel Pond, a mile up the road, more small flocks of phalaropes are flying back and forth over the water. Another flock of thirty-two phalaropes takes refuge in yet another marsh pool opposite Odiorne Point still further north. They present an animated sight indeed, riding the rippled waters close to the leeward shore, facing the sweeping gales off the ocean. I am able to approach to within about 8 feet of them. After considerable time here photographing, I hurry back south to Great Boars Head—but never get there. High tide is still a half hour away but I am driving blindly through a screen of saltwater spray thrown up and over the rocky cliffs at Wallis Sands Beach by the pounding waves. Once I reach Rye North Beach, I can go no further. The shore road at Foss Beach, on the corner of Washington Road, is littered with rocks and debris from the crashing waves, which are breaking through the high, pebbled barriers behind the beach. About 200 yards up Washington Road, trees have fallen across the road. I am resigned to sitting out the hurricane here, about halfway along the 18-mile New Hampshire shoreline.

It is one o'clock, and Hurricane Carol is in full fury. I can neither proceed further south nor reverse to the north. If I stay here on the shore road, there is serious risk of being swept by the storm surge at high tide. I have but one option—drive 100 yards to the higher ground that Washington Road affords. In relative safety, I can now leave the car and devote full attention to the spectacle around me. The strength of the wind is such that I have to lean into it at a 45° angle and force myself to make any progress. Black objects are flying past me like so much debris. I am barely able to pick one up off the ground: black with white rump patch, a Wilson's storm-petrel, still alive. Sadly, when I return to the car with it, the bird succumbs within half an hour. To get there is a battle; the wind forces me to involuntarily run, grab the door handle when I reach the car, and hold on—or fly past it like the birds. I drip from head to toe with salt spray, shingles and roofing paper blow over my head along with at least a dozen storm-petrels—six with the white rump patches—their heads and bodies still facing seaward into the punishing westward wind, no match for the onslaught. Most of them are Wilson's, with a few Leach's perhaps. I am not sure of those without a rump patch, because only two storm-petrels are common off the north Atlantic coast. A neighbor, nailing his screen door nearby, also picks up a petrel and hollers to me to come and get it, if I can reach him, which I decide not to try to do.

The fury of Hurricane Carol. Photograph by Charles Flagg.

The Wilson's storm-petrel is named after that most literary early American ornithologist, Alexander Wilson. The bird also took on the name Mother Carey's chicken from the early sailors off the stormy North Atlantic Coast, a name derived from *Mater Cara*, which means "sweet mother." Unlike the ponderous efforts of the loon and cormorant, who must patter their feet on top of the water to lift off, the smaller swallowlike petrels are experts at pattering and dabbing over the surface of the ocean as they feed. The secret lies in their webbed feet and relatively long wings. It is from this habit that another interesting tidbit surfaces: The derivation of the name petrel comes from the apostle Peter, who "also walked on the water," according to Scripture.

By two-thirty in the afternoon the fury of the hurricane begins to diminish, which is characteristic of these fast-moving storms. Double-crested cormorants—strong flyers—are actually beginning to fly back to the sea with some success. Although normally a thirty- or forty-minute ride, it takes several hours to return to Dover because of the uprooted trees and downed power lines. I see that all the marshes behind the beaches have become vast lakes.

Wilson's storm-petrel. Painting by John James Audubon.

For several days following the storm (1–2 September), a number of black skimmers and Wilson's storm-petrels are seen in Seabrook Harbor, the former resting on the flats, the latter on the water, obviously by-products of the storm. The black skimmers turn out to be a first occurrence for New Hampshire. On 11 September 1954, almost two weeks following Hurricane Carol but only two days after Hurricane Edna (which was much smaller than Carol), for more than a half hour I have the good fortune of watching a Kentucky warbler feeding on the ground within 25 feet of me, on Great Boars Head in Hampton

Kentucky warblers, southern warblers of the type blown in on winds of Hurricane Carol. Photograph by Betty Darling Cottrille, courtesy of the Cornell Laboratory of Ornithology.

Beach. Although not quite a new state record, it is the first record since June 1949 according to Tudor Richards, then the director of the Audubon Society of New Hampshire. On 30 September I observe a blue grosbeak on the same Great Boars Head (a gravel headland, or drumlin, from the last ice age). This species, too, has not been seen in New Hampshire since 1929. Finally, on 5 October, this remarkable 1954 fall migration produces a yellow-throated warbler in the same location, the first in New Hampshire since 1939, again according to expert and friend Tudor Richards. The year 1954 is a remarkable one for southern rarities brought up on the winds of Hurricanes Carol and Edna. These and others, such as the hooded warbler, are reported from Cape Cod and Martha's Vineyard that same autumn, believed to be the result of Hurricane Edna.

How are these birds transported safely during the storm? Apparently, they get caught up in the eye of the hurricane, which as we all know is a large calm area near the center of the storm—think of a hole in a doughnut constantly rotating in a circle. Land birds are deposited on the ground as the storm progresses over land. For southern sea birds, however, terra firma is entirely foreign. They react by trying to get back out to sea and are consequently buffeted by the eastern side of the revolving hurricane winds until they die or are blown exhausted landward again.

Great Boars Head at Hampton Beach was an excellent fall migration site for me in the 1950s and 1960s, often providing the last fall dates for many warbler species. But that was before the proliferation of beach development in the 1970s that essentially eliminated all the vegetation on the headland and dried up my exciting discoveries forever after. Just one more example of humans destroying nature.

Most hurricanes occur in late August and early September. In any given year, as few as a couple to as many as a dozen or more may develop, not all of which will hit land. Incidentally, putting names to these storms became official Weather Service policy around 1953. Only feminine names were used the first few years, but policy changed to include masculine appellations in 1979, thanks largely to the women's movement. Hurricane Carol proved to be one of New England's worst hurricanes, depending on your point of view, since the 1938 hurricane, with which all New England hurricanes are compared. The storm caused almost $400 million (1954) in damage, fifty people were killed, and gusts on the southern New England coast measured 105 to 130 miles per hour.

The 1938 hurricane did its greatest damage inland, running up the Connecticut River Valley, which separates Vermont from New Hampshire, after crossing Long Island Sound, snapping trees off like matchsticks and clearing large swaths of mountainsides. The following ten years or so were bountiful ones for birds that nest in semicleared areas, such as the olive-sided flycatcher, chestnut-sided warbler, winter wren, and many of the woodpeckers. For me, though, the following forty-five years produced few experiences to compare with the awe and excitement of this singular day at the beach.

CHAPTER 16

Music Appreciation

ORNITHOLOGISTS declare dryly that the function of bird song is a pragmatic one: to attract a female for mating and to establish territory to keep out other males. But I think there must be at least one other purpose. It was Ralph Waldo Emerson who said, "If the sages ask thee why this charm is wasted on the earth and sky, tell them, dear, that if eyes were made for seeing, then Beauty is its own excuse for being." Thus, it is a natural extrapolation that if ears were made for hearing, then bird song is also its own excuse for being. It certainly makes a lot of sense. Most singing is a male prerogative we know, but not all. Several females do it too, including the mockingbird, catbird, northern cardinal, house finch, and rose-breasted grosbeak, among others.

A controversy exists regarding songs versus calls. Where do you draw the line? Ornithologists rather arbitrarily do it by considering the length and complexity of the utterance. Calls are apparently innate, whereas, in general, songs are learned. Most birds—even those who do not have the usual songs, like gulls—have a great many call note variations. Songs, too, can consist of several variations. But generally, songs have two main proclamation functions: defense of territory against other males and mate attraction for females. After all is said and done, however, the line between song and call note remains arbitrary in my opinion, at least in many cases, and probably will remain so for a long time to come. The more one looks into the subject, the greater the store of information one turns up, such as the importance of song in bonding, differentiating between neighbors and strangers, affecting the reproductive cycle, and many other subtleties of bird behavior.

Interestingly, scientists also are hung up on terms such as mimicry. The most famous purveyor of that remarkable talent, of course, is the mockingbird. The European starling also has the ability, but in a much reduced repertoire. Why have these birds developed such talents? Ornithologists again speculate that sexual selection has most to do with it, in terms of enhancing mate attraction, stimulation of the female, and intimidation of other males. I suppose this may be true. Also, it seems now that some ornithologists want to change the term mimicry to "vocal appropriation" because of the deceit implied in the word mimicry. Goodness. In the meantime, we really don't have to concern ourselves with these questions to be fascinated by the sheer beauty of the music. The only real problem, as I see it, is the short season of song, two months for the most part.

The thrush family wins any singing contest of North American birds hands down, a declaration with which most birders agree. Many experts have picked their favorite singers through the years. One of the more noted was Arthur A. Allen, the famous Cornell University ornithologist of the first half of the twentieth century, who composed the following list of ten in order of their excellence: hermit thrush, wood thrush, veery, mockingbird, brown thrasher, white-throated sparrow, fox sparrow, robin, song sparrow, and rock wren. Four thrushes and three sparrows! I would drop the brown thrasher and rock wren, and add the eastern meadowlark, the bobolink, and Swainson's thrush. John Burroughs expressed what most birders think: "If we take the quality of melody as a test, the wood thrush, the hermit thrush, and the veery thrush stand at the head of our list of songsters." I agree, except that I would reverse the first two.

In her book *Birdcraft* (1897), Mabel Osgood Wright said, "There is something immaterial and immortal about the song; it inspires a kindred feeling in every one who hears it." No wonder the appellation "swamp angel" was associated with the hermit thrush by early writers. The great John James Audubon never heard the hermit thrush sing because it only does so on its breeding grounds in the Northeast, Northwest, Rocky Mountains, and across Canada from Newfoundland to Alaska, regions in which he never had the good fortune of hearing it sing. Rather amazingly, Audubon badly erred in thinking the bird bred in the Deep South—even Mississippi and Louisiana. Of the hermit

Clockwise from top, the wood thrush, veery, Swainson's thrush, gray-cheeked thrush, and hermit thrush. Painting from the early 1900s by Louis Agassiz Fuertes.

thrush, Audubon (1967, 3:30) stated, "Its song is sometimes agreeable."
Wow! It was the wood thrush, rather, that Audubon swooned over:
"Kind reader, you now see before you my greatest favorite of the feathered tribe of our woods. To it I owe much. How often has it revived my
drooping spirits . . . to cheer my depressed mind (alone in the woods
during a tumultuous thunderstorm), and to make me feel as I did, that
never ought man to despair, whatever may be his situation. The wood
thrush seldom commits a mistake after such a storm; for no sooner
are its sweet notes heard than the heavens gradually clear."

Henry David Thoreau's favorite singer was also the wood thrush.
Apparently, though, Thoreau had trouble separating the wood from
the hermit thrush, and clearly mixed up both songs. This is under-
standable for several reasons: He stopped shooting birds early on and
didn't purchase a field glass until late in life. Thoreau was twenty-eight
when he built his cabin on Walden Pond, at which time he bought a

A hermit thrush. Photograph by Dan Sudia.

telescope, good for water birds sitting still on Walden but not for the smaller land birds on the move. Of the wood thrush, Thoreau wrote: "this sound most adequately expresses the immortal beauty and wildness of the woods . . . all that was ripest and fairest in the wilderness and the wild man is preserved and transmitted to us in the strain of the wood thrush. It is the mediator between barbarism and civilization . . . the gospel according to the wood thrush" (Torrey and Allen 1962). Thomas Nuttall, like many early ornithologists, also confused the hermit with the wood thrush, not to mention what were then known as the gray-cheeked and olive-backed thrushes. (The latter is now known as the Swainson's thrush, and the former is now recognized as two species: Bicknell's and gray-cheeked thrushes.) Tudor Richards heard a unique wood thrush song: "Once in my life I heard a wood thrush sing a continuous song, rather than the usual one with separate phrases, and it was perhaps the most beautiful bird song I've ever heard."

Some of my fondest memories of the hermit thrush, this most gifted singer, are forever linked with blueberry season in late July and August during the 1940s and 1950s. My father would take us blueberrying late on Sunday afternoons in Barrington, New Hampshire, concluding with fishing early in the evening on Swain's Pond (or as it was known in those years, Union Lake). Then we ride back home, where my mother prepares a fish supper while we spread the blueberries on the table and separate the twigs, leaves, and unripe and overripe berries from the good ones. By nine o'clock, supper is ready, but the tastiest fruits of our labor do not appear until the next morning, when, like all good Yankees, a mouthwatering blueberry pie is served as our breakfast. (Actually, this habit of pie for breakfast dates back to our grandmother, on the farm on Knox Marsh Road in Dover, during the Depression. She and my mother were the best pie makers I ever knew, with me a close second, I might add egotistically.) Always the highlight of the day, however, was the ethereal flute sonata of the hermit thrush, which we could count on late in the day no matter how hot it was. I think that experience has to be one reason, at least, for my not disliking the heat of summer as much as other people do.

In the early twentieth century John Burroughs called the song of the hermit thrush the finest *sound* in nature, not just the finest song. High praise. In a delightful little book, *Birds and Flowers about Concord,*

N.H. (1906), Frances Abbott described the feeling that many writers have felt over the years: "There is a peculiarly spiritual quality about the music; and when several hermits were singing in the pines, as they always were on Sunday afternoons, it seemed like an angelic choir in the dim aisles of a cathedral." Or hear what Ned Dearborn had to say in his book *The Birds of Durham and Vicinity* (1903): "Its inspiring song is doubly impressive because it is rendered in the quiet hours of morning and evening, or during the lull following a summer shower, when the clear, soul-stirring melody of this prince of preachers comes up from the somber pines like a benediction." Only three years later, Frances Abbott declared that the pines of Concord, New Hampshire, were gone. A familiar refrain, of course, which continues to send the few remaining birds further and further afield, westward and northward. This may be the reason, along with global warming, why many southern species are moving further north every year.

I suspect those people who consider the song of the wood thrush the most impressive have never heard the hermit sing, for there really is no comparison. The wood thrush's song is a short, rather matter-of-fact *ee-o-lay* with a soft trill at the end, a repeated three- or four-note phrase on the same pitch, whereas the hermit's is repeated more serenely on several, ever-rising pitches. The veery is quite different: a descending spiral of slurred *veer* notes as though uttered through a pipe or echo chamber. The song is mysterious, wild, and wonderful. "Why not call it the echo thrush?" Mabel Osgood Wright (1897) asked. The three remaining thrushes all have a bit of the nasal echo sound of the veery type, but in a different direction. The Swainson's is an ascending spiral of nasal phrases. The gray-cheeked and Bicknell's songs are similar, both somewhat remindful of the veery in nasal quality, but thinner and not the equal of the veery. Bicknell's has a break in the middle with a rising inflection at the end: *chook-chook, weeo, weeo, weeo-titereee.* The gray-cheeked lacks this break in the middle and rise at the end. In his excellent book *A Birder's Guide to New Hampshire* (1996), Delorey stated that the Bicknell's song sounds faster and higher pitched than the slower and lower-pitched gray-cheeked thrush song. In addition, he felt the gray-cheek's song is more disjointed, with more starts and stops than that of the Bicknell's.

The gray-cheeked and Bicknell's thrushes are best identified by their different distribution pattern: extreme northern Canada, from Newfoundland to Alaska, for the gray-cheeked, whereas the Bicknell's is confined to high elevations in New England, the Adirondacks, the mountains of Cape Breton, the Gaspé, and the north shore of the St. Lawrence in eastern Québec. These thrushes can be seen in New Hampshire in late May, while migrating and thus not singing. The two are very difficult to separate visually, but the experts note the warmer brown back of the Bicknell's, which contrasts slightly with the tail, as opposed to the olive-gray back and tail of the gray-cheeked.

I will forever associate the wood thrush with my undergraduate years at the University of New Hampshire in Durham. I spent a great deal of my time reading all the bird books the main library cataloged. I always chose the small cubby next to the windows looking out over the wooded white pine ravine that divided the campus geographically. From that position I could always hear the melodic flute playing of the wood thrush in May near the end of the school year, one of the reasons I never did very well in college; the pull of the birds was just too strong for my weak human nature. The wood thrushes have long since

A veery. Photograph by Dan Sudia.

deserted the campus for the usual reasons, as well as our backyard white pines, which for several years were a consistent locus for a delightful wood thrush concert, but only on a warm, midsummer afternoon following a refreshing rain shower. I always looked forward to these in the middle of summer. Then they stopped abruptly when their nesting woodlot was converted into house lots.

In a different fashion, the veery's haunting pipe dreams, as extraordinary as any sound in nature, are forever associated in my mind with a remote aspen-cattail swamp outside of Woodstock, Vermont, site of an annual pilgrimage to see the equally extraordinary queen lady's-slippers—2000 of them at one time—in full bloom. The veeries were always there tuning up before the heat of the midday sun shut them down in late June and early July. One could hardly wish for a more propitious juxtaposition than that one.

I am fortunate to have seen all five of our spotted thrushes, all in New Hampshire. I encountered the Bicknell's on top of the highest White Mountains: Nancy, Osceola, Cannon, Lafayette, and, of course, the Presidential Range (walking up the Tuckerman Ravine Trail above 3000 feet, where Bicknell's leaves Swainson's behind). Back in the 1950s and 1960s, in the heyday of New Hampshire Audubon field trips with Tudor Richards, the late Kimball Elkins, and others, the Nancy Pond Trail hike at the southern end of Crawford Notch off U.S. Route 302 produced several of the rarer boreal specialties: rusty blackbird, spruce grouse, Philadelphia vireo, both the three-toed and black-backed woodpeckers, and, of course, the Bicknell's thrush above 3000 feet. The Bicknell's was always the premier bird, singing atop a stunted dead spruce, then dropping out of sight into the thick, impenetrable balsam fir and red spruce thickets below, where it was impossible to see. The Crawford Notch area was the base of operations for many eighteenth-century ornithologists and naturalists, including the great Bradford Torrey, one of America's greatest natural history writers.

For those readers who are life-listers, pick up a copy of Alan Delorey's (1996) New Hampshire guide for directions to the most accessible nesting site of the Bicknell's thrush. You can drive up to the site on Jefferson Notch, on the western flank of the Presidential Range; at slightly over 3000 feet, it is the highest elevation of any free public road in New Hampshire. The road to the top of Mount Washington from State Route 16 just north of Pinkham Notch—on the eastern side of the Presidential Range—is a privately owned toll road.

Before we leave the beautiful scenery of the White Mountains of New Hampshire, I must recount a hike up 5260-foot Mount Lafayette in late May 1948. The late Albion Hodgdon led a troop of sophomores from his botany class. We arrived in Franconia Notch in the middle of a cold misty morning, typical of late spring in the mountains, the type of weather that discourages most normal hikers, but not us. It was sunny and cool back in Durham when we started out on the three-hour ride, with the green vegetation well pronounced. By the time we reached the 5000-foot level, the light rain and mist turned to light snow and fog. Other hikers were descending at this point and we followed their lead to avoid any possible mishaps in the cold snow.

The most memorable part of the entire climb—in fact the only thing I remember—was the startling, melodious, ringing, rippling trills of the winter wren that echoed across the vast and dreary dripping landscape, black and gray with leafless trees and slippery moss-covered fallen tree trunks, rocks, and ledges, with nary a hint of the green we left behind in the southern part of the state. No other sound broke the stillness of this now almost morbid (late winter equivalent) mountain landscape, which only weeks before was covered with a mantle of white. Welcome to spring in the notches of the White Mountains of New Hampshire.

On the list of big hitters in the music world of birds, the mockingbird is "the king of song" according to Edward Howe Forbush (1929). He goes on to say, "Perhaps there is no song-bird that the mockingbird cannot imitate to perfection." More than thirty-nine species' songs and fifty call notes have been imitated by a mockingbird; the mimic is so amazingly accurate that an electronic analysis could not detect any difference from the original. In fact, mockingbirds have even improved on some other bird's songs, according to those who know such things, and can imitate a barking dog, the cackling of hens, and whistles of all kinds. Forbush (1929) also noted that W. L. Dawson, of *Birds of California* fame, "heard a mockingbird change his tune 87 times in 7 minutes and that he was able to recognise 58 of the imitations given!" The stories about this bird's prowess are legendary and could easily fill several chapters.

Mockingbirds, one in the spread-winged pose typical of Basil Ede's work. Painting by Basil Ede, courtesy of Basil Ede and the Gulf States Paper Corporation.

Let us now consider some of the lesser singers. The red-eyed vireo is a favorite of mine for two reasons. The male sings all day, even in the hottest part of summer, in a series of deliberate, short phrases repeated exactly the same again and again; the song has been translated as, "You see it. You know it. Do you hear me? Do you believe it?" This bird also holds the record for persistence among North American singers: 22,197 songs in one ten-hour period. (Can you believe they are closely related to shrikes? Red-eyed vireos have a shrikelike hook at the tip of the upper mandible.) Unfortunately, this vireo also has the dubious record for the most cowbird infestations in North America. This species was once the most abundant nesting bird in North America, but it is fast becoming one of the least abundant, not only because of the cowbird parasitism but also because the red-eyed vireo winters in the Amazon Basin of South America (Brazil), whose rain forests are rapidly disappearing.

Other notably persistent singers do not come anywhere near the red-eyed vireo's streak, but are worth mentioning. A song sparrow recorded by the famed Margaret Nice in 1943 sang 2305 songs, although 1500 is more average. A Kirtland's warbler sang 2212 songs—on the day before its first egg hatched, no less. Finally, a black-throated green warbler sang 1680 songs in one seven-hour period. It takes a patient observer to sit and record for so long a time, a task that not many have done.

Most people would not think of the wood-pewee as much of a singer. In the early 1900s, however, Gene Stratton-Porter (of *Girl of the Limberlost* and *Freckles* fame) thought otherwise: "The professional 'wailer' of the forest is the wood pewee, and I should like to engage him to 'wail' at my funeral, I would ask no finer music. There is no sadness in their song, they have composed a song in harmony with their surroundings; but to our ears this music contains the notes with which we express solitude, silence and heartbreak. Long-drawn, clear, aching with melody, through the solemn silence of the forest, high above you comes his *pee-a-wee*."

In her book *Music of the Wild* (1910), Stratton-Porter proclaimed the male eastern meadowlark (even more so the western) as the most popular singer and "the bird of the people," not because of his musical superiority, which he does not have, but because he is the first to sing in the spring, at the first hint of green in field and meadow. The fact that his breast is covered with the choicest of gold doesn't hurt his case either. Two ringing whistles, translated as "Come here! Spring o' the year!" or "See you, See air," comprise the song of the meadowlark. In the perfect prose of Mabel Osgood Wright (1897): "A breezy sound, as fresh and wild as if the wind were blowing through a flute." Around here, however, it is more difficult each year to catch a breath of that fresh air. I fear there is only one place left in my hometown to experience this wonderful sound of spring.

Luckily, in 1986 a land trust bought and preserved one of the few remaining coastal farms on the southern Maine coast. Laudholm Farm, within view of the Atlantic Ocean in Wells, Maine, just off U.S. Route 1, is the place to go now for both the meadowlark and bobolink. The Laudholm farmhouse itself is a rare survivor of Greek Revival architecture. The 1600 acres of field, forest, wetland, marshes, and beach are part of the Wells National Estuarine Research Reserve, a 4-mile-long natural ecosystem of tidal and river marshes along the coast. Other coastal estuary preserves are being established along our New England coast, in the nick of time, to save these few remaining, extremely valuable ecosystems from further draining and development. A few miles south of the Wells reserve, in Newington, New Hampshire, the Great Bay National Estuarine Research Reserve was established in 1989 and encompasses the new Great Bay National Wildlife Refuge at the western end of the former Pease Air Force Base.

Back to the sounds of music, now, with the bobolink, who embodies the farmer's hayfields during May and June. This bird soars above in an ebullient flutter of joyous, bubbling melody, *bob-o-link*, *spink*, *spink*, *spink*, then suddenly disappears among the grasses. Again and again, the bobolink repeats his courting display to show off his handsome black and gold uniform conspicuously complimented with white rump and scapulars. Fewer farms and early mowing make for a bleaker future for this former favorite of the barnyard, except in the few reserves mentioned previously. At least restaurants no longer serve this "reed-bird, four on a skewer for fifty cents." It's true, in the late 1800s bobolinks and other songbirds were gunned down for the markets. Admittedly, however, in those years millions of bobolinks and other blackbirds raised havoc in the rice fields on their long autumn journey to Argentina (more than 5000 miles), causing extreme crop damage. Rice farming has since declined and hunting stopped, but the bobolinks never fully recovered.

Shooting practice came to a halt in 1918 with the passage of the Migratory Bird Treaty Act signed by Canada and the United States. It took another eighteen years for Mexico to join the pact. With the exception of waterfowl and certain upland game birds (for which specified hunting seasons are allowed), these treaties effectively protect all the birds of North America. You may be interested to know, however, that the nonnative house sparrow and starling (both introduced from England), are exempted, that is, shooting these two species is legal.

When I really want to revel in the nostalgia of such open-country favorites as the bluebird and meadowlark, in May and June I head for the northeast kingdom of Vermont, between Peacham and Lyndonville, where I can renew many of my orchid acquaintances at the same time. It is an ideal overnight trip. In bygone years, Vermont proudly claimed more cows within its borders than people. With the accelerating farm foreclosures of the past couple of decades, however, the state can no longer make that claim. Fortunately, open space is still plentiful in the Green Mountain State and cows remain a part of its pastoral scenery. In New Hampshire in the late 1800s agriculture was such a large part of the state's economy that our forests were stripped for more pasture and fields until less than 10 percent remained. A hundred years later, the regeneration of the forest is nearly 80 percent complete; because of the continuing decline of that same farm economy, nature has slowly reclaimed the land left idle. These forests are all second and third growth, of course, punctuated with large and small development, which diminishes the possibility of extensive, contiguous patches of mature forest ever existing again.

It will not win any singing contests, but the loud, whistled *whip-poor-will* song always thrilled my senses as a child. Mabel Osgood Wright (1897) called the whip-poor-will a "weird bird," listing it under the songless bird section of her book *Birdcraft*. Others also consider the whip-poor-will's song merely a call, but however one chooses to refer to it, the sound remains one of my most vivid memories of the Maine woods as a child of twelve. Unfortunately, I haven't heard the whip-poor-will for far too many years, for the same reasons, of course:

overdevelopment, rapid loss of open space and habitat, and the general suburbanization of rural areas.

Another member of the nightjar family, the common nighthawk, is not a hawk at all, but a cousin of the whip-poor-will. Again, the nighthawk's sounds are not what we would call a song, I suppose. One must look to the sky on a warm summer night at dusk and early evening to hear those two sounds. One is a nasal *peent* call as it flies or darts through the air erratically on long wings—high and low—scooping up insects in its cavernous mouth. The *peent* carries a long distance. After hearing this sound, eyes still on the sky, you will see the nighthawk suddenly dive-bomb—the male's courtship display—near the bottom of which the wings make a loud muffled *boom*, followed quickly by a resonant, rising *swr-r-r-onk* as the air vibrates his primaries and the bird pulls out of the dive.

Who can ever forget the call of the common loon on a northern wilderness lake in June? The loud, wailing, yodeling breaks the silence like nothing else in the great outdoors, a never-to-be-forgotten sound. Mostly, one must travel to northern parts of our border states or Canada to hear the loon, along with that other magnificent voice of the mountains, the winter wren. I hear this marvelous song on Squam Lake, New Hampshire, occasionally even as late as August, on my weekly trips to Holderness for the three-birds orchid (*Triphora trianthophora*), which also occasionally blooms during that month. But that's another story you will have to pick up in my *Wild Orchids Across North America* (Keenan 1998). The loon's penetrating call is made up of several *hoo, hoo, hoo* notes in a vibrating tremolo, or yodel. The sound is supposedly easy to imitate to call up the bird, but not by me. You really have to hear it to believe it—truly astounding. With all the recent books and tapes on the subject, one can enjoy the wilderness experience vicariously sitting at home. But, believe me, that's nothing compared to the actual experience on a northern lake.

CHAPTER 17

An Introduction to Nests

THE DIVERSITY in life applies to just about anything you can think of: animals, plants, even cars, clothes, and entertainment in our world of built-in obsolescence. But some things rarely change—like bird nests. Certainly, there is great variety, but little change from year to year in any species' nest design unless the usual building materials at the disposal of the particular bird are missing from time to time. There are even field guides to identifying nests, such as Hal Harrison's *A Field Guide to Birds Nests* (1975). Also, I suggest reading John K. Terres's monumental *The Audubon Society Encyclopedia of North American Birds* (1980), which presents an intriguing compendium of facts.

How is this for variety? Around the corner from our house, a Baltimore oriole's typical bag nest is suspended from the pendulous tip of an American elm tree, with two or three long strands of silver Christmas tinsel at the bottom blowing in the breeze. A pair of robins build a nest, a typically large mud bowl, not on the usual tree branch or crotch but right on top of a tree swallow house nailed to the side of our house under the roof overhang. Then there was the late summer (and second brood) when our annual pair of house wrens decided to use our cotton clothes-pin bag hanging on the metal line on the back lawn. What made it so useful for this purpose, I suspect, was the fact that the bag was half full of clothes pins, which provided a nice platform for the eggs and young and made the bag more accessible through the opening at the top.

Nests range from nothing more than a scrape in beach sand (piping plovers and oystercatchers), bare ground and flat roofs (common

A highly unusual Baltimore oriole's hanging nest, which incorporated several strands of silver Christmas tinsel, in an increasingly rare American elm tree on a local city street. Dover, New Hampshire, 1996.

This house wren confiscated a homemade clothes-pin bag on our clothesline to successfully raise a second late-season family. Dover, New Hampshire, 26 June 1988.

This camouflaged killdeer sitting on a nest of wood chips successfully raised her family in a roped-off display area of Tuttle's Farm garden center, the oldest family farm in America. Dover, New Hampshire, May 1996.

A veery nest and eggs on the ground. Barrington, New Hampshire, June 1984.

nighthawks), and bare rocks of cliffs (auks and murres) to the platform nests at the tops of dead trees (herons and hawks) and the so-called adherent nests of chimney swifts, which are glued with saliva to the vertical wall of a chimney. Similarly, barn and cliff swallows affix their nests with mud under the eaves of various structures. Then there are the cavities that woodpeckers dig in trees and belted kingfishers and bank swallows burrow in banks of clay and sand. The most common type of nest, however, is built by songbirds: the cup nest. The largest of any North American nest is made by the bald eagle, the smallest that of various hummingbirds.

Altricial birds produce young who are naked at birth and require extensive time in the nest, whereas precocial birds are ready to leave the nest in just a matter of hours and partially feed themselves. The latter category includes the ducks, gulls, and gallinaceous (chickenlike) birds whose young are chicks (grouse, pheasant, and other game birds). Margaret Nice, the song-sparrow expert, did a study of altricial birds (Terres 1980). She compared the success rates of hole-nesting species

A cliff swallow building a mud nest under an eave of a building on the grounds of Fundy National Park visitor's center. New Brunswick, Canada, July 1985.

(66 percent) to those who use open nests either on the ground or in vegetation (49 percent). The smaller success rate of open nesters probably explains why they tend to have more broods in a season, to offset these losses.

Cowbirds belong to the troupial family, which is another name for the Icteridae (Greek for "jaundice," or "yellow green"). The family includes blackbirds, orioles, meadowlarks, and the bobolink as well as cowbirds. We all know what a parasite cowbirds (specifically, the brownheaded cowbird) are to other songbirds. At least 214 species are known to have been parasitized by the brown-headed cowbird. Of this number, 121 have raised the young cowbirds to maturity with or without their own nestlings surviving in the same nest. The most heavily victimized species are the yellow warbler and song sparrow. The least victimized are the hole-nesting birds, such as woodpeckers, chickadees, and bluebirds. Some hosts, such as the cardinal and yellow-breasted chat, will desert their nest and rebuild. Others, such as the American robin and gray catbird, have been known to throw the cowbird eggs

A ruffed grouse nest and eggs on the ground. Photograph taken with a flash. Rye, New Hampshire, 30 May 1954.

out of the nest, while others in some cases build a floor over the cowbirds eggs before laying their own. As many as six layers have been built by the yellow warbler in an attempt to discourage the intruder, and all six layers contained some cowbird eggs. Persistence again, a game of who will outlast the other. The female cowbird often will carry the owner's eggs away from the nest and eat their contents, including the shell.

How do these nefarious birds find the nests? Simply by keeping a close watch in the springtime and watching the victim build its nest, which can take up to a week or more, then visiting the nest in the dim light of predawn and laying her eggs before the host bird begins to incubate her own clutch. Sounds like the potential for a television mystery thriller. Herbert Friedman (1971) stated his opinion that the cowbird's dependent habit may have originated when it lost its motivation to defend territory. This idea seems a bit far-fetched to me. Whatever the reason, thankfully cowbirds are the only North American birds that practice this habit.

An ovenbird nest and eggs on the ground. White Lake State Park, Ossipee, New Hampshire, June 1984.

Ninety percent of the nests I discover are essentially by accident, in conjunction with doing something else like hiking, botanizing, or taking photographs. Most birds are close sitters, that is, they do not flush from the nest until almost stepped on. In that case, careful investigation of the immediate surroundings will often disclose the nest. Some, however, such as the meadowlarks and bobolink, almost always run away from the nest over the ground before flying off, in which case it is of little help to note where the bird was flushed. Most nests are generally well hidden from view. And some, like that of the ovenbird, are obscured under extraneous debris, which is usually evidenced by a domelike appearance over the nest. In almost all cases, what I find is a nest full of eggs and no fledglings. Once, however, I found a black-capped chickadee nest in a hole at the top of a dead stub about 5 feet above the ground. When I first noticed the adult leave the stub, I discreetly inspected the hole to see what was there. Eggs, as usual, but

A vireo or warbler nest in a vibrant red maple sapling at the end of the nesting season or even later, demonstrating the strength and stability of the nesting material in the crotch. Madbury Reservoir, Madbury, New Hampshire, 11 October 1971.

now I could return a week or so later and be assured of finding young ones. To the utter amazement of me and my young son, Greg, a half dozen wonderful coal black little bundles of down, all compressed in the bottom of the hole, stared up at us without moving a muscle. To this day, one side of me despairs in not taking the time to photograph the scene properly, but I did not have the heart to disturb the young or the parents any longer than the few seconds it took to look down the hole. Good etiquette should always win out. With ground nests, it is difficult to pinpoint their location when returning a week later, without risking tipping off a predator or a fellow human by flagging the spot, which is a definite no-no.

A most amusing situation occurred on Kodiak Island off the southern Alaska coast. Returning to Kodiak City from an orchid field trip at the southern end of the island on the only road, we passed a bald eagle's nest right beside the road, about 40 or 50 feet up in a tree. Both parents sat side by side like comic caricatures, barely contained by the

A slate-colored junco nest and eggs on the ground. Parker Mountain, Strafford, New Hampshire, 24 May 1997.

nest, eyeing us attentively as we drove by without stopping. In the 1980s, I took an impromptu hike looking for wild orchids on Hick's Hill, a small drumlin in Madbury, New Hampshire. I accidentally discovered a rare example of nesting by a goshawk near the New Hampshire coast on top of the hill. Each of my follow-up visits were punctuated by attacks of the hawk swooping down at me in long sallies from the nesting tree, narrowly missing my head each time, a typical demonstration of parental protection and a thrilling experience for me. Standing motionless, I had plenty of time to react while watching it swoop through the trees on a beeline course toward me.

Common terns successfully nested on the beach and dunes of Hampton Harbor and Salisbury Beach on the New Hampshire shore every summer for years, until the real estate explosion of the 1960s and 1970s produced far more people and dogs than terns, effectively destroying any further opportunity to raise a family and insuring the rapid decline of these fabulous flyers in most of New England. (Gull depredations on island nesting grounds had a similar effect.) Unlike the goshawk's method, the terns would attack by dive-bombing me in the open, while keeping up a constant bedlam of angry and raucous *kee-yarr* and *kuk-kuk kuk* calls, just inches from my head. Like the hawk, however, there was never a direct hit.

Some species use the same nest each year. These tend to be the largest birds, such as the bald eagle, osprey, and some hawks. Records for ospreys and peregrine falcons, for example, indicate the same nest was used annually for 50 years or more. Some birds do not build a nest, but simply appropriate a neighbor's instead. The great horned owl is a case in point, using the nests of great blue herons, hawks, squirrels, or crows. Most, but not all, songbirds (passerines) build new nests each year. H. E. McClure (1944) reported that of 489 nests studied in Iowa, the three best and strongest built belonged to the American robin, Baltimore oriole, and mourning dove, which may explain why these three species often reuse their nests from year to year.

Although many birds lay white eggs, some lay colored ones. One theory suggests that most birds who lay white eggs are hole nesters (in trees or in the ground) such as woodpeckers, owls, and kingfishers. Even though white eggs are more conspicuous than colored or dark eggs, it matters not at all for a cavity nester. Most birds, however, lay their eggs in open nests exposed to predators, and dull, speckled, and even colored eggs are less noticeable to predators. Having said this, it is true that some hole nesters, such as the eastern bluebird, wrens, and chickadees, do lay colored eggs, and some open air nesters, such as herons, ducks, and gallinaceous birds (for example, grouse and quail), lay white eggs. In the latter case, these birds always cover their eggs with grasses and other plant material before leaving the nest unattended, which both camouflages and incubates the eggs. Perhaps the ovenbird, who lays colored eggs, covers its nest with plant materials for this incubation benefit.

In closing, I must comment on the practice carried on by some ornithologists and collectors of yesteryear. Before laws were enacted to prevent the habit, collectors not only shot, stuffed, and displayed birds in their own homes and museums, they also took eggs from nests to put on display. R. C. Banks et al. (1973) came up with an astounding bit of information regarding this early practice: As of 1969, a total of 4.2 million bird skins and 638,840 nests and/or eggs were residing in 283 institutions and private collections in North America. You read it correctly, the figure is *4.2 million*. Now, of course, only scientific collecting is permitted, but, quite frankly, I question the need for that in North America except in extremely rare circumstances.

CHAPTER 18

Tools of the Trade

B IRDING is one of those pastimes that doesn't require you to spend a lot of money to have a lot of fun. With a field guide and a good pair of binoculars, you are off and running. Actually this is merely the tip of the iceberg, as they say. Unfortunately, when you reach my age (over sixty-five) previously unforeseen things can often cloud the picture, literally. Two of the most important are cataracts and hearing loss, both of which usually come on gradually. In my case, however, I lost my entire high-pitched capabilities in basic training at Fort Dix, New Jersey, during the Korean War. In those years, earplugs were not a standard issue to recruits on the rifle range. As a consequence, each evening in the mess hall, I was unable to hear the conversation of the person sitting directly across the table from me. This condition gradually wore off during the evening, so that by morning I was again able to hear normally, or so I thought, until I went birding again and discovered I no longer heard the high-pitched notes of the warblers. Once discharged from the Army, I was given a hearing test that confirmed what I knew in the field: The upper range of my hearing was now severely impaired. In those years, one accepted his fate automatically. My hearing loss was especially disheartening, however, because up until those two years in the service, I had mastered the identification of the warblers by song—no easy feat. One of the first and one of my favorites was the buzzing *zee zee zee-zoo-zee* of the black-throated green, originating from the highest branches of whispering white pines in a favored woodlot, ten minutes from my home, now long since destroyed for development. Such cutting continues unabated, resulting in fewer and fewer opportunities for those still able

to hear these wonderful sounds. It was easier in those days to connect
to the words of Thoreau:

> For I'd rather be thy child
> And pupil in the forest wild,
> Than be the king of men elsewhere.
> To have one moment of thy dawn.
> Than share the city's year forlorn.

I learned to live with this partial hearing loss during the ensuing
forty-five years, but sorely missed the ability each spring and summer
to locate birds hidden in vegetation by sound before sight, which all
birders learn to do early on—a great advantage. At various times over
the years, I had my ears tested by an audiologist, who verified the
upper-range loss but also acknowledged that my conversational hearing did not require a hearing aid. Each time, I was permitted to use the
device on a trial basis, only to return it because it did not help. Even
with my ear against a compact-disk player's speaker, no warbler sounds
came through. Recently, however, I read about a new technology in
Birding Magazine, the quarterly journal of the American Birding Association. This device is called Walker's Nature Ear, which claims to bring
back these lost sounds, at the amazing cost of only $200, substantially
less than other hearing aids. Unfortunately, the device barely made a
difference in the field. Only when I placed my ear against the speaker
in the house did I hear my first warbler songs in forty-five years.

I must also report that since the purchase of the Walker device two
years ago, my hearing has begun another cycle of loss, wherein the
red-eyed vireo, hermit thrush, even the robin and scarlet tanager are
more difficult to hear unless they are nearby. Nature Ear is helping
with some wonderful songs, however, so there is hope for me and the
rest of you in the same boat. For some reason, I do not read much
about hearing impairment in the birding press—perhaps because
there is limited success with all hearing aids. But it is an increasing
problem that will only get worse, with a population exposed to such
high decibels at one time or another in our lives. The remarkable
Helen Keller, when asked which handicap was the hardest to live with,
stated without hesitation that her deafness was the most difficult for
the simple reason that the gift of hearing bonded people together

socially more closely than that of sight. This is a thought-provoking insight, although I think I would favor sight if presented with the same choice.

Two years ago I had my first cataract operation on the right eye and knew the left eye was just a matter of time. I constantly compared both eyes by alternately blocking them with the palm of my hand. The difference is significant in terms of sharpness, except when my good eye is blurred with occasional floaters that have developed since the first cataract operation, a condition, I am assured, that has nothing to do with the operation and afflicts a sizable number of people who have never had cataract surgery, including my best friend and optometrist, Dr. Raymond Alie, of Hampton, New Hampshire. There appears to be no good reason to delay the second operation. Quality of life will certainly be enhanced, and the odds are 95 percent in my favor.

As a birder, I am always interested in which binoculars people use. In 1945 I was fortunate to receive a pair of 7×50 Zeiss World War II glasses that my older brother Tom brought back from Germany, following his service in the war as a combat engineer. For about the next fifty years, these glasses were always superior to any I compared them with. They took a great deal of abuse, too, in all kinds of weather. But I committed the cardinal sin of cleaning the lenses with whatever happened to be at hand—a handkerchief or paper napkin. Actually, it amazes me how long they performed so well. Finally, the scratches caught up with me, and a few years ago I had to buy my first new pair of binoculars.

Any glass is only as good as the person's eyes, so the binocular obviously will not deliver its full potential. However, I must mention a factor that I overlooked when I bought the new pair, the 10×50 Celestron Ultima, an excellent binocular except for one key element: close focus. After comparing this binocular with several other brands, I bought it on the basis of superior optical sharpness and brightness. But, alas, I had neglected that all important close-focus ability, which in the Ultima was a very disappointing 25 feet. I gave these to another member of the family not as interested in birds and hastened to buy the Bausch and Lomb Elite 8×40, which focus down to an incredible 6 feet. What a pleasure.

The most popular binoculars for birders are the 7×35 category. When you get into the 10×50 range, you are talking about a heftier weight and price. Then there is the question of porro prism (the older, traditional design) versus roof prism (more compact, with straight barrels). It's valuable to try several out, preferably in the field rather than in the store, and don't make the mistake I made. Of course, the quality of the optics is the most important thing, and one cannot expect the best for less. The old cliche "you get what you pay for" is not always true, but it is more often than not when purchasing a good glass. Expect to pay between $500 and $1000 for the better and best. Some of us, however, cannot afford or are unwilling to pay for the best, and, actually, there are some good values to be found. The Bushnell 8×42 Natureview (under $100) and Swift Plover 8×40 (under $200) both focus to 10 feet or so. According to Stephen Ingraham (1998), the

Some of my birding equipment. Left to right, clockwise: Sigma 400-mm telephoto lens, APO f 5.6; Sigma 70–300-mm zoom, auto-focusing, APO f 4.0–5.6 macro lens; World War II–vintage Zeiss 7×50 binoculars; Bausch and Lomb 1950s–vintage spotting scope; Elite 8×42 roof-prism binoculars; Canon extension tube EF 25. Not shown is my Canon 35-mm EOS single-lens reflex camera with a 100-mm EF 2.8 macro lens, which took this picture and most others in this book.

expert binocular researcher for *Birding Magazine*, the Bausch and Lomb 8 × 36 custom (around $250) and the Opticron Imagic 8 × 42 (around $180) both provide the "same kind of optical performance as a $1000 roof." Finally, for what it's worth, my limited experience with compact glasses in general has not been very good. In my opinion, when choosing a glass to observe birds with, size is the least important factor to consider.

Although I have a conventional old Bausch and Lomb spotting scope, your next paycheck should go for one of the new scopes that feature zoom eyepieces. According to Steve Ingraham (1998), the following are among the best of the new zooms: Nikon Fieldscope 78-mm ED, Kowa Fluorite TSN-824, Swarovski AT80HD, Bausch and Lomb 77-mm Elite ED, Swift NightHawk 80-mm ED, and Celestron Ultima 80-mm. The advantages of a good zoom lens are obvious. Before the era of good zooms, birders had to put up with screwing on and off the eyepiece as many as three times, most of the time losing sight of the birds in the process.

Let me say a few words about bird photography. Even though I took most of the photographs in this book, I never invested the money in professional equipment, such as costly lenses in the 500- and 600-mm range (and even higher) recommended by some pros for superior results. These lenses can cost as much as $10,000 to $15,000. The bare minimum focal length recommended by most professionals is a 300- or 400-mm telephoto. Also, teleconverters can be used to increase the magnifying power of those lenses. Suffice it to say that I followed Thoreau's suggestion when it came to bird photography—simplify. Consequently, most of the time I get along with my Canon EOS10S single-lens reflex and a Sigma APO 70–300-mm zoom. Furthermore, almost none of my pictures were taken with a flash. I prefer pictures with natural light and at least some real habitat ambience, avoiding as much as possible the posed studio look with black or other uniform background. I used both Fujichrome and Kodachrome films (100 and 200 ASA, generally), the camera supported mostly by a tripod or bean bag on a car window and sometimes hand-held by necessity of the situation. For those of you who are interested in the more complex photographic aspects of birding and have the money to spend, one of the better books is Arthur Morris's *The Art of Bird Photography: A Guide to*

Professional Techniques (1998). For you generalist nature lovers, look up my book *Wild Orchids Across North America* (Keenan 1998) for more detailed opinions on wildflower photography. As I have often said, it is difficult to do birding and botanizing together: one requires constant looking up, the other constant looking down, as well as different lenses.

The field guide solution is much easier than some of the other decisions for the first-time birder. Most birders prefer the National Geographic Society's *Field Guide to the Birds of North America* (1999). More than 1 million copies have been sold since the first edition appeared in 1983, thus reinforcing its position as perhaps the number one field guide. The American Bird Conservancy's *All the Birds of North America* (1997) features a different concept that emphasizes habitats; in general, the paintings in this book are superior to the other field guides, in my opinion. After being brought up on the traditional Peterson system, which is based on field marks, *All the Birds* takes a bit of getting used to. Of course, Peterson's *A Field Guide to the Birds* (1980) is still out there (in eastern and western editions), as are the Stokes's (1996a, 1996b) field guides, which use photographs instead of paintings. Most people seem to prefer paintings, believing them to be more accurate in details.

For nearly fifty years I relied on the Peterson system, but I now use the National Geographic Society's (1999) field guide more often, partly because of the continental coverage and thus the convenience of vast information in one volume, a decided advantage, especially if your birding is more than regional in nature, which it will be some day if it is not already. Nonetheless, it was the late Roger Tory Peterson who developed and honed the concept of field marks in his first edition, which was published in 1934. Peterson changed forever the way people studied birds, taking it out of the purview of scientists and into the world of everyday birders. Whereas more than twenty different artists painted the birds in the National Geographic book, Peterson alone did those in his. Approaching ninety, Peterson died while working on the fifth edition of his unprecedented field guide, because, he said, "it has not been done well enough yet."

Once you expand your travel horizon, another indispensable thing you will need is the series of American Birding Association/Lane bird-finding guides. The one on southeastern Arizona (Taylor 1995), quite frankly, is the best regional bird-finding guide I've ever seen and used. The series covers most of the best birding areas in the country, with more on the way, including revised editions. For those of you who want to start a bird book collection at some point, part of chapter 20 is devoted to my favorite bird books.

How to keep warm is always a good question, although it applies to winter birding more than any other. Most people agree that the warmest boots are the Canadian-made Sorels. (Their only drawback seems to be their bulkiness, which can interfere with driving.) Most people recommend more than one pair of socks: a wool outer and a wicking inner liner. Of course, you have to allow for this when buying the boots, otherwise they will be too roomy when only one pair is worn, which happens under some situations. These will keep you warm and dry under most conditions, except in deep snow that comes up above the

Birders on the observation platform at Cape May Point State Park. Cape May, New Jersey, 4 October 1994.

top of the boot and filters down inside the sock or edge of the boot. Gore-tex and similar waterproofing materials are essential for hiking in the rain and water. Although these materials work well, they are not fully protective, obviously, when the water is above the boot and trickles down. Wellington boots are useless also when the water is over the edge, which is precisely why some people are happy with plain old sneakers under these conditions. I own a pair of Asolo light hiking boots, which have served quite admirably year-round. I seldom have problems, and I know of many people who prefer hiking up mountains and sloshing through swamps with nothing but sneakers on, not worrying one tweet about wet feet. The point is there are trade-offs in everything, so do not worry about fashions, looks, or what others think.

Which brings to mind how things were forty or fifty years ago when I started all of this. We've come a long way since those days when it was considered somewhat suspect (or sissified) for a guy to have a pair of binoculars in hand, bird-watching on the side of the road. At the approach of a car or one of your peers, the first impulse was to walk away and hide or in some way pretend to be doing something else, thinking fast on how to deflect the inevitable put-downs. It just was not cool in those days to be known as a bird-watcher. In fact, I was always athletically inclined. I participated in three sports in high school and had an older brother who was all-state in high school football. But when it came to my playing football, I took a calculated risk, choosing not to participate because it interfered with the fall migration season. I did play with those same team members before and after the season in pickup games (without such equipment as a helmet) and actually was better than most of them. (I just had to get that in there.)

CHAPTER 19

The Evolution of Bird Painting

S INCE THE beginning of my interest in birds at age ten, paintings and illustrations were my inspirations to acquire and collect bird books. The desire to know the names of the artists was just as strong then as the desire to know the names of every living thing I came across. I always wondered why the artists were not given their just due on the printed page. Historically, with a few exceptions like John James Audubon, the artist's credit most often appears in small print on the title page, buried in the acknowledgments, or not at all. As a photographer, I notice this all the time: the photographer's name in the tiny type along the lower outside edge of the picture or, worse, buried on the inside edge near the spine of the book or magazine, where it often requires bearing down on the pages to expose the name. Why? The artwork is an integral part of the manuscript, and the artist deserves prominent recognition. Indeed, in some cases the artwork is the only good reason to buy the book, especially if it is in color. (When depicting nature, with rare exceptions, color is the only way to go, in my opinion.) It follows, then, that this interest should properly lead to a chapter on artists from the perspective of an admitted amateur critic with a deep and abiding love for the painters of birds. I actually own most of the books mentioned, so my opinions are based on personal experience with the material.

Experts seem to agree that the two greatest American bird painters of all time are John James Audubon (1785–1851) and Louis Agassiz Fuertes (1874–1927). In the 1930s several painters (or illustrators) began to appear on center stage, such as Roger Tory Peterson (1908–1996), but the jury, of course, is still assessing the work of these modern artists. From the standpoint of accuracy in the living bird, there is no doubt that Fuertes's rendition of birds is quite superior to Audubon's. One must remember, however, that Audubon started from scratch, so to speak, with few examples of other work, whereas Fuertes built on a foundation of predecessors and peers. Actually, Alexander Wilson (1776–1824) and Mark Catesby (1682–1749) both preceded Audubon, but they were no match. Wilson's and Catesby's paintings

John James Audubon (1785–1851). Portrait by Nicola Marshall, courtesy of the Kentucky Department of Parks, John James Audubon Museum.

were more typical of the work of European artists at the time: archaic, stiff, and lifeless, drawn as they were from stuffed specimens. At any rate, the hierarchy of American artists is delineated by some authorities in the following manner: Mark Catesby was the founder of American ornithology, William Bartram (1739–1823) the grandfather, Alexander Wilson the father, and John James Audubon the patron saint.

Audubon was sometimes characterized as irresponsible, inconsiderate, and impractical, with little or no business acumen. Yet, as Roger Tory Peterson (Peterson and Peterson 1993) noted, "The former bankrupt businessman became a super salesman, traveling from city to city (in Europe) to secure subscriptions; as a sort of production manager, he monitored with infinite care the work of the engravers and a corps of colorists. . . . He was not only artist, author, and scientist but also publisher, business manager, treasurer, and bill collector. How could he have been 'irresponsible' or 'impractical' if he could do all this?" The engraver Robert Havell Jr. of London, who collaborated with Audubon over a twelve-year period on his un-

precedented masterpiece, *The Birds of America*, is considered Audubon's artistic equal for his work in transcribing the original paintings. In fact, Havell even changed some of the paintings by adding or subtracting certain details during the engraving process.

Audubon's massive book measured 29.5 × 39.5 inches and weighed more than 50 pounds, the largest book ever published up to that time (1827–1838). Two hundred sets of this double-elephant folio edition (which are the engraved prints by Havell) were bound and sold by subscription. The book consisted of 435 life-size prints representing 1000 birds, at a subscription price of $1000 each, a very expensive item in those

Alexander Wilson (1776–1824). Portrait by Rembrandt Peale.

days. Twelve years after his death in 1851, Lucy Audubon, his widow, sold the original paintings to the New York Historical Society, where they can still be seen today. Remarkably, of the 200 original bound engraved sets, 134 have survived intact: 94 in the United States, 17 in England, and 23 in twelve other countries, according to an extraordinary piece of scholarship by Waldeman H. Fries. Twenty-eight sets were broken up, 11 were destroyed by fire or war, parts of 14 incomplete sets exist, and the remaining 13 are unaccounted for. It has taken a hundred years for any payoff in the Audubon collector's market. As recently as 1920 a complete set sold for $2500, a little more than double the original investment. After World War II, prices sharply escalated to $18,000, and reached $60,000 in 1960. Then the lid blew off: Complete folios sold for $400,000 in 1977 and several million dollars in the early 1990s.

Audubon produced a smaller and more affordable version of his masterpiece, called the octavo (an eighth of a whole sheet of paper,

Blue-winged teals in flight, revealing the showy blue epaulets. Painting by John James Audubon.

usually resulting in a 6 × 9.5-inch book). This edition consisted of seven volumes produced between 1840 and 1844, and the printing of 1200 copies soon sold out. Several more reprints and editions have continued to appear down to the present day, although these later editions varied a great deal in terms of quality color reproduction.

In March 1994 I had the good fortune to attend an exhibition of ninety of Audubon's original paintings and the truly colossal double-elephant folio (on display under glass in the middle of a room) at the Museum of Fine Arts in Boston. Among my favorite Audubon paintings are his barn swallow, blue jay, white-crowned sparrow, Baltimore oriole, common tern, blue-winged teal, snow bunting, rose-breasted grosbeak, and white-winged crossbill. You will note almost all are "action shots."

Louis Agassiz Fuertes is considered the finest painter of birds of the first quarter of the twentieth century and in some minds the entire century. His life ended tragically at the age of fifty-three, when his auto was struck by a train, thus ending a brilliant career that had the potential for eclipsing any other bird artist in history. Like many bird painters, Fuertes was considered by some experts primarily an illustrator or bird portraitist. It has been said that he had difficulty with landscapes (you couldn't prove it by me). However, even the great Audubon hired apprentices to do his backgrounds: Names like Joseph Mason, George Lehman, and Maria Martin come to mind, as well as his two sons, John W. and Victor Audubon.

Fuertes illustrated many books, but never wrote one. His first commission was for Mabel Osgood Wright's *Birdcraft* in 1897. Fuertes did these portraits in 1895 and 1896, at the ripe old age of twenty-one. One of his most famous commissions involved the three-volume set on the *Birds of Massachusetts and Other New England States* by Edward Howe Forbush (1925–1929), the books I spent the most time with at the library in high school and college, before I accumulated the money to buy them. Because of Fuertes's unfortunate death in 1927, the plates in the third volume were never finished (Major Allan Brooks completed the project). Fuertes probably attained the most acclaim with the fabulously popular one-volume *Birds of America* (1917), edited by T. Gilbert Pearson, which went through multiple printings during the 1930s and 1940s. Upon receiving it as a Christmas gift from

Louis Agassiz Fuertes in his laboratory at Cornell University with his painting *Duck Hawk* in the background. Photograph courtesy of The Cornell University Library.

Black-backed woodpeckers. Painting by Louis Agassiz Fuertes.

my mother in 1941, Pearson's book became my first and chief source of information. The paintings in this book were reproduced from the earlier two-volume *Birds of New York* (1910, 1914) by E. Howard Eaton. Fuertes's woodpecker paintings remain favorites of mine, especially those of the three-toed and pileated. His "Gyrfalcon and Kill in Snow" is spectacular. Then there is another classic, the two-volume *The Bird Life of Texas* (1974) by Harry Oberholzer, which shows Fuertes at the pinnacle of his brief career. His paintings of the western kingbird, vermilion flycatcher, and Lewis's woodpecker are exceptional.

The man who finished the Massachusetts set, Major Allan Brooks, was a retired officer in the Canadian army. His warblers in the Forbush set have heads that are too large and rounded, while the tails are short and upswept, resulting in an unnatural arc. In his later work, it became apparent that Brooks corrected some of these shortcomings. Nobody is perfect, of course, and I do like many of his paintings: the swallow-tailed kite in *The Hawks of North America* (May 1935), for example. Brooks was a staff painter for the National Geographic Society, illus-

Gambel's quail. Painting from the early 1900s by Louis Agassiz Fuertes.

trating the two-volume *Water, Prey, and Game Birds of North America* (1965) with Walter A. Weber (1906–1979), another staff member. In general, I prefer Weber's work to Brooks's and cannot think of a better painting of the ivory-billed woodpecker than Weber's two-page spread in the aforementioned set. Many of his warblers are also superior to those painted by Brooks. Some people think Weber's long association with the society limited his potential as one of the greatest artists of this century.

Bruce Horsfall (1868–1948) was a contemporary of Fuertes and Brooks. His credits span countless nature magazine pages, including *Bird-lore* (the precursor of today's *Audubon Magazine*), various Audubon Society projects, and such books as Frank Chapman's *The Warblers of North America* (1907; also illustrated with early Fuertes examples) and Alice E. Ball's *American Land Birds* (1936). Horsfall also painted habitat backgrounds in exhibits at the American Museum of Natural History in New York City (as did Francis Lee Jacques a little later). I like the familiar, even old-fashioned (late Victorian style) quality of Horsfall's impressionistic scenes, particularly examples of his chickadees and juncos, both with snowy backgrounds. The three-dimensional effect created by adding a second or third bird to the interior of the scene is not seen much today, because many contemporary artists are illustrating strictly for identification and not esthetics, largely due to budget constraints. In his early work, Horsfall had less success with warblers, but the same can be said about many other bird artists, including Audubon and Fuertes. In general, though, he is not in the same class as most of the twentieth-century bird artists. One bird-art critic went so far as to describe Horsfall's art as "saccharine sentiment," which perhaps explains his lack of popularity today after a great deal of success the first half of the twentieth century.

I first became aware of Rex Brasher (1869–1960) through his pen-and-ink drawings for Pearson's *Birds of America*. After much publicity and prolific output in the 1920s, his appeal declined rather precipitously, despite living to the ripe old age of ninety-one. His original work can still be seen, however, in the Connecticut State Museum of Natural History at Storrs. A biography by his nephew in the 1960s includes several examples of bold close-ups of larger species like the California condor and clapper rail, which do not appeal to me at all.

A warbler medley by Walter Weber. From top to bottom: Cape May, golden-winged, blackburnian, magnolia. Painting courtesy of the estate of Walter Weber.

Francis Lee Jacques (1887–1969) was commissioned by the great Frank Chapman of the American Museum of Natural History to paint backgrounds for stuffed animals and birds. His main legacy, perhaps, are these dioramas in three different locations: the Peabody Museum at Yale University, the Museum of Science in Boston, and the American Museum of Natural History in New York City. Waterfowl paintings and other larger birds, in general, were Jacques's specialty, whereas some of the smaller birds—especially warblers—fared relatively poorly, as was the case with other painters previously mentioned. Jacques had a distinctive style; "Cypress Backwater" and "Sea Duck" are two outstanding examples in *South Carolina Bird Life* (Sprunt and Chamberlain 1949) and *Florida Bird Life* (Sprunt 1954). But the best examples are in one of my all-time favorite books, a biography by his wife, Florence Page Jacques, eloquently produced and titled *Francis Lee Jacques: Artist of the Wilderness* (1973). Black-billed magpie, hooded merganser, wood duck, and a lone pronghorn antelope (sorry, I know it is not a bird) are wonderful examples of his unique style and skill in handling backgrounds.

George Miksch Sutton (1898–1982) was an academic at three universities: Cornell, Michigan, and Oklahoma. As such, he was torn between the many disciplines of teacher, author, explorer, and bird painter, which reduced his artistic output and creativity. Sutton enjoyed his accomplishments in the teaching profession more than anything else. He was a favorite protege of Fuertes, and some have called him the dean of American artists—and not just because of his age. With few exceptions, I do not care for his numerous head portraits and other bare poses, however, the painted redstart and red-faced warbler in the *Birds of Arizona* (Phillips et al. 1964) are fine pieces.

John Henry Dick (1919–1995) is one of the few, proud owners of Audubon's double-elephant folio. He is also one of the few who photographed Bachman's warbler before it disappeared from the swamps of South Carolina, the species apparently now extinct like the ivory-billed woodpecker. Dick stopped painting years ago because of eye problems, but not before illustrating another of my favorite books, *The Warblers of North America* (Griscom and Sprunt 1957). The paintings were done in 1955, and when compared to the 1948 paintings done for an earlier book, *Florida Bird Life* (Sprunt 1954), the difference of seven years is amazing. Not all of Dick's paintings are outstanding, but those of the bay-breasted and blackpoll, prothonotary, magnolia, and red-faced are the best warbler reproductions I've seen.

Arthur Singer (1917–1990) specialized in illustrating field guides, like the Golden Guide to *Birds of North America* (Singer 1983). *Birds of the World* (Austin 1961), however, is a coffee-table book. In my opinion, Singer came closest to the style of Fuertes than anyone else of his era.

In addition to being one of the last to see the ivory-billed woodpecker alive, Don Eckelberry (b. 1921) is noted for the 1948 three-volume set of field guides he illustrated with Richard Pough for the Audubon Society. Regretfully, he then shifted his work to Trinidad and the West Indies for tropical birds, seeming to drop out of the American scene. Despite a relatively small output (at least I have not seen much of it), Eckelberry is considered one of the all-time greats in talent and technical knowledge. Two of my favorite Eckelberry paintings are a close-up of six black skimmers on a white-sand beach and a flock of red-breasted mergansers flying low over the water with surf and rocks in the background.

The iconoclastic Robert Clem (b. 1933), of *The Shorebirds of North America* (Stout 1967) fame, no longer paints for book reproduction. As a result, a mint copy of this book is now selling for several hundred dollars on the used-book market. Independent and a perfectionist, Clem now paints only originals to please himself, shunning even the limited-edition market and refusing to follow the dictates of clients. His favorite subject remains shorebirds and the environment. *The Shorebirds* never appealed to me for two main reasons: a similar treatment of every subject—not a single bird in flight throughout thirty-two plates in this coffee-table volume—and too many of the birds look as if they were stuck in the sand or artificially placed on a rock.

In contrast to Clem, Robert Bateman (b. 1930) puts many of his birds in flight, notably the "Peregrine Falcon Chasing Turnstones," an excellent panoramic in his 1985 book, *The World of Robert Bateman*. His close-up painting of the hooded merganser is also excellent. (The fact that these birds are my favorite duck helps.) Like many of the high-priced waterfowl carvers of the day, Bateman's work represents the modern approach of showing minute feather details. Roger Tory Peterson was quoted as saying, "If I could paint like another wildlife artist, it would be Robert Bateman." What more is there to say?

J. Fenwick Lansdowne (b. 1937), somewhat like his compatriot Robert Bateman, paints with extremely delicate detail—one can almost count the individual feathers. By the time he was in his early thirties, he had several coffee-table books under his belt, including the notable two-volume set *Birds of the Eastern Forest* (Lansdowne 1968, 1970) and *Rails of the World* (Ripley 1977). Here again, some of Lansdowne's warblers are disproportioned in terms of upswept tail and hunched head. Having said that, however, other warblers are perfectly rendered, such as the black-and-white warbler against white birch bark and the redstart. Lansdowne's scarlet tanager and rose-breasted grosbeak are two more outstanding renditions.

Kenneth Carlson is best known for his work in *Birds of Western North America* (Carlson 1974). Most of this work includes little background material, but the pair of elegant trogons in an Arizona sycamore is one of the best I've seen of that species. Carlson's work has been compared to Fenwick Lansdowne's.

The Birds of Canada (Godfrey 1986) features the paintings of John Crosby, senior artist of the National Museum of Canada. Crosby's work is first-rate, were it not for the intrusive number placed beside each bird on every plate in the book—too bad. His scissor-tailed flycatcher is the best I've seen, although I think this bird deserved a plate of its own.

Like many bird painters and wildlife artists, William Zimmerman is noted most for his waterfowl work. He has also illustrated three state books: Indiana, Illinois, and Ohio. The one I like the best, though, is the deluxe edition of Arthur Cleveland Bent and Zimmerman's *Life Histories of North American Woodpeckers* (1992), which was intended to be the first in a series of reprints of Bent's entire multivolume set of *Life Histories of North American Birds*, with the addition of color paintings by Zimmerman and the deletion of the original black-and-white section at the end of each book. The project apparently never made it beyond this first volume. Despite the uniformly dreary tan backgrounds, the acorn, red-headed, pileated, and ivory-billed woodpeckers are beautifully done. For whatever reason, more artists seem to do their best painting with members of the family Picidae.

Larry McQueen is one of the newer painters that have caught my eye and interest. Bold use of color and thick brush strokes are typical of his style. The American Bird Conservancy's *All the Birds of North*

America (1997) features McQueen in the warbler section; his paintings are among the best ever done for this group, in my opinion. He is currently collaborating on works of Colombian and Peruvian birds.

For a distinctive view of American birds by a Brit, one cannot go wrong with *The Art of Basil Ede: Wild Birds of America* (1991). Born in England in 1931, Ede became a full-time painter in the 1960s. He began the paintings for this book in 1975 after a chance meeting with Jack Warner of the Gulf States Paper Corporation in Tuscaloosa, Alabama, who went on to financially support this fifteen-year project. (This set up was sort of the reversal of John James Audubon seeking support for his monumental work in England nearly 150 years earlier.) I enjoy the animated subjects characteristic of Ede's art.

Guy Tudor is a portraitist of world renown, working mostly with South American birds and, thus, theoretically outside the parameters of this book. He is currently collaborating with Robert Ridgely on a four-volume set depicting all the birds of South America, having already completed the separate *Birds of Venezuela*. I include him here for personal reasons: In August 1999, Tudor called to request help in seeing the three-birds orchid (*Triphora trianthophora*) in bloom at Squam Lake, New Hampshire, having read about this unique orchid in my book *Wild Orchids Across North America* (Keenan 1998). Incidentally, Bob Ridgely's father, Beverly, has written two editions of *Birds of the Squam Lake Region*, a copy of which I own and have enjoyed on my trips to Squam Lake during the past twenty years.

We come now to the foremost artist-birder-ornithologist of the twentieth century. To these titles we can add writer, photographer, educator, and conservationist. You know his name, of course, everyone does. Roger Tory Peterson (1908–1996) is called the founder of the environmental movement because he made natural history (read "birds") accessible to the general public in a way unsurpassed by any individual in history, through a revolutionary system of field marks, beginning with his 1934 *A Field Guide to the Birds*. The Peterson field guides are world-renowned and have gone through countless printings and several editions, for both eastern and western North America. Just before his death at age eighty-seven, he was single-handedly working on yet a new edition. (By contrast, the second edition of the well-received National Geographic field guide enlisted the help of sixteen

Yellow-shafted flickers. Painting by Basil Ede, courtesy of Basil Ede and the Gulf States Paper Corporation.

artists and thirty other contributors. Rather incredible.) Peterson always lamented the time required to do the guides, saying it was "like sweating blood." So why did he continue doing it so late in his life? Because the previous editions were not "perfect," he said, and needed redoing, a reflection of his perfectionist temperament.

Peterson's large paintings of birds reflect that perfectionism and precision to the point of being almost too pretty and posed. Peterson was commissioned by Mill Pond Press to do beautiful bird portraits to be hung on walls. His birds are like wedding portraits, perfectly composed, male and female the center of attention, bouquet wired, nothing out of place. But I do like much of the work he did for books: *Birds of Newfoundland* (Peters and Burleigh 1951) is an early work of merit that is hard to find today on the used-book counters. Despite the problem of crowding too many birds on one plate, which is so typical of most state and regional books because of economics, I like the blue-winged teal group, which displays the blue patch better than most; the redstart; and the snow bunting and horned lark plate. Unlike most painters, Peterson became a noted bird photographer as well—penguins were a specialty and his favorite bird. He also was an excellent writer, the classic *Wild America* (Peterson and Fisher 1955) spurred my interest in southeastern Arizona early on.

By the way, it is interesting to remember that Chester Reed's truly pocket-sized bird guides were used by the inimitable Roger Tory Peterson and his group of birders early in their careers. Reed's books can be considered the precursor to the modern guide introduced by Peterson in 1934. In 1914 Reed also published a full-sized book on birds, called simply *The Bird Book*.

This survey of bird artwork barely touches on the work of many of the great artists. Unfortunately, many fine artists are left out, such as Beadle, Gilbert, Ripper, House, and Pratt, to name a few. My choices, preferences, and opinions are obviously subjective and from the perspective of an amateur, but there is nothing wrong with that. I hope this chapter may stimulate some of you to begin a collection of a few of the world's most beautiful books ever published, just as I have done. You will be glad you did.

CHAPTER 20

Favorite Birds, Books, and Photographs

H ERE, I LIST a baker's dozen of my favorite birds. Granted, the difficulty of picking favorites of anything is more than a lot of people care to indulge in, but I have always enjoyed picking favorites in just about any category one proposes.

1. American redstart: the essence of flash, exuberance, and joy in microcosm;
2. hermit thrush: North America's sweetest flutist;
3. hooded merganser: arguably the fairest of the fowl;
4. scissor-tailed flycatcher: the essence of beauty and grace;
5. pileated woodpecker: with the demise of the ivory-billed, the king of the woodpeckers;
6. roadrunner: the desert is never a lonely place with this bird around;
7. swallow-tailed kite: remarkable fork-tailed aerial gymnast in boldest black and white;
8. roseate spoonbill: the most distinctive, heavenly pink wader;
9. black-capped chickadee: dependable, year-round member of the family at the feeder;
10. American robin: the world would be a duller place without its glorious early morning serenades;
11. prothonotary warbler: makes the darkest and scariest swamp come to life with its luminous golden flash;
12. blue-winged teal: the blue wing epaulets of a flock wheeling in unison is one of nature's more remarkable and memorable sights;

13. willet: the bold black-and-white wing pattern, coupled with its loud and ringing *pill-will-willet* call, transforms the drabbest northern marsh in May.

Over the years, I have gradually accumulated a substantial library of natural history books and magazines. In addition to my favorite artists discussed in chapter 19, I thought some readers might be interested to learn about some of my favorite books and photographs. Also, for three excellent articles listing "the best books" and how to build a library of old and new books, see the October 1976 issue of *American Birds*, the February 1993 issue of *Birding*, and the April 1994 issue of *Birding Magazine*.

Before I begin, however, I want to relay the true story of a remarkable man. Emanuel Rudy Rudolph was a botany professor at Ohio

A roseate spoonbill, undoubtedly one of our most beautiful birds. Photograph by Dan Sudia.

State University until his retirement in the early 1990s. Rudolph loved books and kept accumulating them to the point where he was running out of space in his house. So, what did he do? To the amazement of his colleagues, he actually bought the house next door (in Columbus, Ohio) to accommodate all of his books, more than 53,000 volumes in his personal library. Understandably, he was in great demand by library groups and bibliophiles and he received many honors and appreciations. Then, out of the blue, he died in a tragic auto accident, leaving more than 50,000 books for his wife to deal with. It's one of the most amazing stories I ever read. I came across it by accident at the University of New Hampshire Biology Library, in a lengthy remembrance written for the *Torrey Botanical Club Bulletin* (April–June 1993). Every time I think of it. . . . Well, back to my story.

Field guides for identification are well represented since the Peterson system first appeared in 1934. I grew up using almost the entire collection of books as they appeared. Several editions of Peterson's *A Field Guide to the Birds*, both eastern and western, were the first, best, and longest in personal use. My list of recommendations also includes Arthur Singer's *Birds of North America* (1983), the third edition of the National Geographic Society's *A Field Guide to the Birds of North America* (1999), Stokes and Stokes's (1996a, 1996b) eastern and western guides, and the American Bird Conservancy's *All the Birds of North America* (1997). Take your pick, noting that the National Geographic Society's and American Bird Conservancy's are the only recent one-volume guides to all North American birds north of Mexico. Also, the Stokes's guides use photographs, whereas the others are illustrated with paintings.

The newest field guide on the market is *The Sibley Guide to Birds* (2000), the much-acclaimed book written and illustrated by David Sibley. Let me say up front that the book is oversized and too large to carry into the field, at least for many people (even birders), and is likely to be left in the vehicle. For most birders, especially beginners, the third edition of the National Geographic Society's field guide or Peterson's are better choices in the field. Sibley's, however, is the most detailed by far of the so-called field guides, and the book makes for profitable and pleasant reading at home. Unfortunately, the colors of many species are not accurate. A personal example came to my attention this winter, when for the first time in more than twenty years we had several dozen purple finches at our feeder, along with the rather ubiquitous house finches. The relatively difficult distinction between the purple finch and house finch requires careful color comparisons. In Sibley's guide the colors are the same, and he does not show the distinctive dull raspberry color of the male purple finch and the bold creamy and brown head stripes of the female purple finch. In other examples, the reds of the towhees, thrashers, and robins are bright scarlet—much too much so—and the blue tones are off. Another strong distraction to me was the distortion in length of many of the smaller land birds' wings as shown in flight. The larger birds, however, such as the water birds and hawks, are rendered very well. The book's price is a bargain, and most reviewers call it the best guide to the birds yet. In fact, David Sibley did everything in the book himself—paintings, text, and maps—an achievement unique in the bird world, as far as I know. Even Roger Tory Peterson never accomplished that.

Older books that were an early inspiration include E. H. Forbush's three-volume *Birds of Massachusetts and Other New England States* (1925–1929). Before I earned enough money to purchase my own set, during high school and college I spent hours at a time in various libraries. Most of the paintings were done by Louis Agassiz Fuertes, except for some of the smaller birds, which makes for some unevenness in quality of the art. In my opinion, Eaton's *Birds of New York* (1910, 1914) contains the best of Fuertes's work, with different and better plates than the Massachusetts volumes. However, as with many things in life, there are trade-offs to make: The prose of Forbush is not to be missed, and, in general, Forbush's three-volume set is the better book. Arthur Cleveland Bent's classic *Life Histories of North American Birds* evolved into twenty-six volumes between 1919 and 1968, a massive undertaking unsurpassed by anyone before or since. Of course, the volumes are missing some information from the past forty years or so, but will always have a place in my collection and should in yours.

Because warblers are my favorite family of birds (who would have guessed?), several of my favorite books include them. The best of the older books is Frank Chapman's *The Warblers of North America* (1907), which includes some of Fuertes's relatively unimpressive early work. I spent a great deal of time with a used copy of this book in the 1940s and 1950s, until I was able to identify all the warblers by sound and sight in all plumages. Then, the appearance of Griscom and Sprunt's *The Warblers of America* (1957) really teased my taste. The illustrations by John Henry Dick are superb for the most part, an improvement over his previous work in such things as *Florida Bird Life* (Sprunt 1954) and *South Carolina Bird Life* (Sprunt and Chamberlain 1949); the latter two books are good showcases, however, for Francis Lee Jacques's artistic talents.

Curson, Quinn, and Beadle's *Warblers of the Americas: An Identification Guide* (1994) describes and illustrates—with paintings—all of the wood warblers including those in Central and South America. I also must mention Hal Harrison's *Wood Warblers World* (1984) and, of course, A. C. Bent's monumental *Life Histories of North American Birds* (the wood warbler volume was published in 1953). For behavior and ecological studies on warblers, consult Douglass H. Morse's *American Warblers* (1989), which has an excellent photograph of a singing common yellow-throat on the jacket. Dunn and Garrett's (1997) Peterson field guide series on warblers probably contains the most diverse and comprehensive information on the species to date, as well as offering two kinds of illustrations—the paintings are very good, the photographs only average.

For the best warbler photographs (of all fifty-two species) and an entertaining narrative on how they got their pictures, be sure to pick up a copy of Vera and Bob Thornton's *Chasing Warblers* (1999). Eric Salsman, a reviewer for the American Birding Association, in a capsule review of the book in the October 1999 *Winging It* refers to the photographs as "rather variable in quality," an astounding opinion to me. I feel they are the best ever done on American warblers. Barth Schorre's *The Wood Warblers* (1998) is a smaller paperback edition. Although the photographs in Schorre's book are good, they cannot compete with the Thorntons' photographs because too many of them are taken on the same lichen-covered twig with identical poses. Also, many of the photographs in *The Wood Warblers* were taken by other photographers, which, in my opinion, makes the book less remarkable than the Thorntons'.

For more fantastic warbler photographs, see Winston Williams's *Birds of the Northeast* (1989), which presents the work of Barth Schorre,

Michael Hopiak, and Robert Simpson. The redstart images, for example, including spread wings and tail, are the best I've seen. A companion volume of Williams's on the *Water Birds of the Northeast* (1989) has an excellent shot of a flock of blue-winged teals that illustrates my earlier point about the striking beauty of flocks of this duck in flight.

Herbert Brandt's *Arizona and Its Bird Life* (1951) did more to spur my interest in so-called Mexican birds, which cross the border in the extreme southwestern United States, than anything else in the literature. Although a bit verbose and repetitive for some modern tastes, there is much of interest, including wonderful paintings by George Miksch Sutton, Roger Tory Peterson, and Major Allan Brooks. It also displays the most beautiful book cover of any bird book I am aware of: pebble-surfaced, dark green simulated leather, with a richly embossed gold roadrunner emblazoned below the gold title. It's worth having just for the cover, in my opinion. I bought Brandt's book for $15 when it was published in 1951, and it is now an expensive item on the used-book market.

Outstanding biographies of two of the best modern-day bird artists are *Francis Lee Jacques: Artist of the Wilderness* (1973) by Florence Page Jacques and *Roger Tory Peterson: The Art and Photography of the World's Foremost Birder* (1994), edited by Peterson and Rudy Hoglund. To put a face and story to the names of dozens of birds with eponyms of pioneering ornithologists, look for Barbara and Richard Mearns's *Audubon to Xantus* (1992), a remarkable achievement that makes the sport and history of birding so much more rewarding.

For a handy, important, but weighty one-volume research tool, I like John K. Terres's *The Audubon Society Encyclopedia of North American Birds* (1980). Unfortunately, the arrangement of photographs is such that quick page access to many entries is annoyingly slow at times. But the photographs themselves are top-notch in most cases. Terres's tremendous bibliography contains many excellent books on the ecology and conservation of birds—remarkable scholarship here.

Two of the better anthologies are Peterson's *The Bird Watcher's Anthology* (1957) and Peattie's *A Gathering of Birds* (1939). Peattie's book includes more biographical material on the respective authors, but has fewer excerpts. John Terres's *Things Precious and Wild* (1991) is a book of nature quotations from Edward Abbey to Ann Zwinger, a veritable smorgasbord of delights. *The Nature Reader* (1996), edited by Daniel Halpren and Dan Frank, has the added benefit of a favorite reading list of natural history books, annotated by a distinguished group of advisory editors.

Finally, some memorable photography has been published in *Audubon* and *National Wildlife* magazines, two of the longest running, most consistently beautiful, award-winning natural history magazines. A real collector's item is the January 1978 issue of *Audubon*, called "Audubon's Ark," which commemorates the Audubon Society's eightieth anniversary and recounts its many successes in the sanctuary business. A two-page spread of the roseate spoonbill by Philip Kahl highlights that beautiful issue, which also includes Kahl's superb black-crowned night-heron. In the April/May 1984 issue of *National Wildlife* magazine, Michael Smith's bluebirds (piled inside a bird house on a winter night) struck me as one of the most unusual bird photographs I've ever seen. Judging by the number of reproductions of the image over the succeeding years, the photograph has made a great deal of money for Smith. Another *National Wildlife* issue, the October/November 1985, features three of Art Wolfe's notable owls: hawk, snowy, and great gray.

CHAPTER 21

Extinction Is Forever

T HE MOST astonishing story I ever read about birds appeared
many years ago in the anthology *A Gathering of Birds* (1939)
by Donald Culross Peattie. Taken from Alexander Wilson's
American Ornithology (1808 and beyond), the subject involved that
king of all American woodpeckers, the ivory-billed:

> The first place I observed this bird at was about twelve miles
> north of Wilmington, North Carolina. Having wounded it
> slightly in the wing, on being caught, it uttered a loudly reiter-
> ated and most piteous note, exactly resembling the violent cry-
> ing of a young child, which terrified my horse so, as nearly to
> have cost me my life. I carried it under cover to the streets of
> Wilmington where its affecting cries surprised every one with
> looks of alarm and anxiety, thinking it a child. Procuring a room
> after divulging the nature of the package, which transformed
> the astonishment to laughter, I locked him in my room while
> taking leave to put up my horse. In less than an hour I returned,
> and as I opened the door, he set up the same distressing shout,
> which now appeared to proceed from grief that he had been dis-
> covered in his attempts at escape. He had mounted along the
> side of the window, nearly as high as the ceiling, a little below
> which he had begun to break through. The bed was covered
> with large pieces of plaster; the lath was exposed for at least
> fifteen inches square, and a hole, large enough to admit the fist,
> opened to the weather-boards; so that in less than another hour
> he would certainly have succeeded in making his way through.

I now tied him to the table before going off to seek food for him (I wished to preserve his life) and upon returning, I heard him again hard at work, and on entering had the mortification to perceive that he had almost entirely ruined the mahogany table to which he was fastened, and on which he had wreaked his whole vengeance.

He cut me severely in several places, and displayed such a noble and unconquerable spirit, that I was frequently tempted to restore him to his native woods. He lived with me nearly three days, but refused all sustenance, and I witnessed his death with regret.

This astonishing story is forever etched in my mind, and I have reread it many times since that initial reading many years ago. It reinforces a strong admiration for and interest in one of the most remark-

An ivory-billed woodpecker. Painting by Walter Weber, courtesy of the National Park Service.

able birds, a bird that I will never see. Unfortunately, the ivory-billed woodpecker is now extinct, due, in part, to the lack of sentiment and shortsightedness of American policymakers, notably Franklin D. Roosevelt, who in 1943 rejected a last-minute appeal by the National Audubon Society to save the last known tract of wilderness the ivory-billed still survived in, the Singer Tract near the town of Tallulah, in northeastern Louisiana. Roosevelt is considered historically as a conservationist. One may rationalize, therefore, that because the country was at war, neither Roosevelt nor Congress had the time for this kind of distraction.

The late James Tanner did his Ph.D. dissertation on the ivory-billed woodpecker at Cornell University in the late 1930s. He still found five on the Singer Tract in 1941, calling as loud as ever. But Don Eckelberry, a great painter of birds in his time, was the last ornithologist to have authentically documented seeing the bird in the United States, in April 1944 in northeastern Louisiana. The ornithologist John V. Dennis claimed to have seen a female in the Big Thicket of eastern Texas as late as December 1966. A few qualified others are sure of sightings as recently as 1985. Most other recent sightings, however, are clearly misidentifications. (As Clifford Shackleford, a biologist for the Texas Parks and Wildlife, put it: "If an ivorybill were worth $100 a sighting, we'd have a lot more ivorybills.") The ivory-billed woodpecker measured nearly 2 feet in length and had a wingspan of nearly 3 feet. The bill was ivory white and the all-white secondaries were visible in flight and at rest. The pileated woodpecker differs in several significant ways: It is several inches smaller, has a dark or black bill, lacks the broad white wing patches while at rest, and the female has a large white underwing patch. Julie Zickefoose (1999), an artist, interviewed several birders about their impressions of the ivory-billed woodpecker and wrote a marvelous, surprisingly upbeat article.

As Zickefoose said, "No holy grail has been more sought after on this continent, or aroused more rumors or recriminations, than this bird." Today, there are more than 1 million acres of state and national wildlife refuges in Louisiana alone. I remember very clearly the desperate attempts a few individuals made to find surviving ivory-billed woodpeckers in the 1940s and 1950s. Even newspapers carried these stories for years. In this present day and age, policies are changing for

A pileated woodpecker. Notice the definitive differences in the wings and bill coloration of this and the ivory-billed woodpecker. Painting by Walter Weber, courtesy of the estate of Walter Weber.

A pileated woodpecker at work. Notice the large holes these birds make. Photograph by Mike McHugh, courtesy of the Cornell Laboratory of Ornithology.

the better: With the establishment of the Environmental Protection Agency even the tiny, insignificant snail darter carried enough clout to hold up a giant hydroelectric project a few years ago.

Let us consider, then, the reasons for the extinction of the ivory-bill. Certainly, the mass draining of swamps, the continued exorbitant development of river and lake frontage, and the insatiable appetite for timber—in a nutshell, the enormous destruction of habitat—were leading causes. Still, there are thousands of acres of suitable riparian swamp habitat remaining, albeit widely separated. The ivory-billed woodpecker apparently required up to 2000 acres (or 3 square miles) of undisturbed forest to raise and feed a family, mostly on long-horned beetles. (The pileated has adapted to much smaller woodlots and carpenter ants.) This largest of all our woodpeckers used its "ivory dagger" to superficially scale off the outer bark of the tree for these beetles, whereas the smaller pileated chisels deep, rectangular holes. The pileated was nearly as bad off as the ivory-billed around the turn of the twentieth century, when clear-cutting almost completely denuded the landscape. The species has recovered remarkably in the past few decades, however, with the return of the forest, the demise of eastern agriculture, and its requirement of less territory.

The early ornithologists knew exactly where to find these American icons: almost exclusively along the coastal plain swamps from southeastern North Carolina along the Santee River in coastal South Carolina through most of Florida and Louisiana to extreme eastern Texas (The Big Thicket) and upriver along the Mississippi to its confluence with the Ohio. In those early years, our natural resources seemingly endless, collecting birds by shotgun and egg collecting were the norm. Hunters and squatters also contributed to the demise of the ivory-billed woodpecker, drawn by the loud, clear, plaintive call notes, heard at great distances and, of course, the size of this unique bird.

Around 1850, Audubon clearly saw the handwriting on the wall, and he warned of the inevitable result of this unlimited shooting: "Travelers of all nations are fond of possessing the upper part of the head and the bill of the male, and I have frequently remarked, that on a steamboat's reaching what we call a wooding-place, the strangers were very apt to pay a quarter of a dollar for two or three heads of this woodpecker." Also, Native Americans come in for their share of the blame. Audubon continues, "I have seen entire belts of Indian chiefs closely ornamented with the tufts and bills of this species, and have observed that a great value is frequently put upon them." It was said Indians believed that these body parts transmitted the virtues of the bird: the great courage, beauty, and size. The southern Indians supplied the demand for the tremendous bills and the feathers, which were held in such high esteem by northern tribes. Then there are the directors of museums, who wantonly increased the number of their specimens. It is hard to believe that in some southern museums the number of stuffed ivory-bills reaches into the hundreds. So it went, on and on, until the final too little, too late attempts to stop the hemorrhaging. It sounds so familiar even today.

It was only late in life that Audubon himself came to realize that Americans were killing without regard for the future. Earlier, he had boasted many times of shooting more than a hundred birds in a day, much more than he needed for painting or research. Some authors call him obsessed with shooting, "in blood up to his elbows," a trait that could be applied to most of his peers, it would be fair to say. It must be remembered, however, that in Audubon's time there were no national parks, wildlife refuges, conservationists, or even hunting laws; the markets were full of birds of every description and size, including sparrows and robins. His obvious guilty conscience surfaced many times in his writings, but his "love of Science" always won out in the field. But awareness often results in concern, which is followed by action, and that was the case during Audubon's later years, marking him as one of the first conservationists. At least that is one of the arguments supporting the use of his name by one of the foremost conservation organizations in the twentieth century.

Alexander Wilson was born in Scotland in 1776, nine years ahead of Audubon's birth in Haiti in 1785. Both Wilson and Audubon lived part of their lives in the Philadelphia area, then considered the hub of intellectual thought and activity; both were self-taught artists who quickly fell in love with birds; and both traveled a great deal, seeking bird specimens to paint. In the early 1800s they each decided to paint all the known birds in America, although Wilson predated Audubon in this endeavor. In one of the strangest juxtapositions of its kind, Wilson met Audubon (neither had ever heard of the other) in Audubon's Henderson, Kentucky, store in 1810, while soliciting subscriptions for his multivolume epic. Audubon, in turn, showed Wilson some of his work. It is easy to empathize with the feelings that must have permeated Wilson upon seeing Audubon's work, when he had believed that he had no rival. In his diary, Wilson acknowledged that Audubon's pictures were "very good." Ten years later, Audubon decided to embark on his own venture with *The Birds of America.* The struggling Wilson, jilted by three women and under great stress, died four years later in 1824, at the age of forty-eight. Thus, the stage was left for Audubon.

In his preface to *The Birds of America* (1840), Audubon had this to say about Wilson: "The ornithology of the United States may be said to have been commenced by Alexander Wilson, whose premature death prevented him from completing his labors. It is unnecessary for me to say how well he performed the task which he had imposed upon himself; for all naturalists, and many who do not aspire to the name, acknowledge his great merits."

Whereas the ivory-billed woodpecker was common in the coastal plain swamps of the Southeast and up the Mississippi River to the junction of the Ohio, the only appropriate word for the passenger pigeon was superabundant. In 1813, near Louisville, Kentucky, Audubon exclaimed:

> The multitudes of wild pigeons in our woods are astonishing. The air was literally filled with pigeons; the light of noon-day was obscured as by an eclipse; the dung fell in spots, not unlike melting flakes of snow; and the continued buzz of wings had a tendency to lull my senses to repose. The pigeons continued to pass in undiminished numbers for three days in succession. Not a single bird alighted; for not a nut or acorn was that year to be seen in the neighborhood. The banks of the Ohio were crowded with men and boys, incessantly shooting. Multitudes were thus destroyed. For a week or more, the population fed on no other flesh than that of pigeons, and talked of nothing but pigeons. The pigeons were picked up and piled in heaps, until each had as many as he could possibly dispose of, when the hogs were let loose to feed on the remainder.

Audubon describes other slaughters at the pigeon's roosting sites, shooting ever more wagonloads of the birds. In fact, on a daily basis hundreds of barrels of their corpses were shipped to New York City alone. Nothing was off limits, even their nesting sites. It was like killing the goose that lays the golden egg. Audubon said, "Here again, the tyrant of the creation, man, interferes, disturbing the harmony of this peaceful scene. As the young birds grow up, the trees are felled, in such a way that vast quantities are destroyed." The passenger pigeon laid only one or two eggs, usually one of each sex. With such wanton killing, it is little wonder that before the end of the nineteenth century what seemed like inexhaustible flocks were reduced to merely a handful of birds. And then, none were left—the last survivor died in the Cincinnati Zoo in 1914. We do not have to ponder the reasons for this magnificent bird's demise. There was really only one.

A pair of passenger pigeons. Painting from the early 1900s by Louis Agassiz Fuertes.

As with the ivory-billed woodpecker and pileated woodpecker, the passenger pigeon had its own relative look-alike that still survives abundantly today, thanks to the elimination of hunting pressures. Unlike the other doves, the mourning dove is a permanent resident (although still partly migratory) in the lower forty-eight states, except in the most northern parts of the states bordering Canada. The mourning dove is smaller than the passenger pigeon was, with less bulk and a shorter tail; also, the upperparts from head to tail are brown instead of bluish gray.

More than eighty species of birds have become extinct since the 1600s, with the vast majority of extinctions occurring in the 1800s and 1900s. Today, more than that number are on the endangered species list. We are all familiar with some other names, such as the great auk, heath hen, Labrador duck, Carolina parakeet, all long ago perished from the scene. Bachman's warbler, the Eskimo curlew, and several others will probably soon be added to this roll call. In fact, the rate of extinction is accelerating, due in part to extensive habitat destruction in wintering grounds in Central and South America. These birds are some of the wild heroes of the environmental movement. There are a few human heroes, of course, led by such names as Robert Marshall and Howard Zahnister (Wilderness Act of 1964), Aldo Leopold, Rachel Carson, and Stewart Udall, who said "The great depression was a bill collector sent by nature." Indeed, we have made some strides to stem the tide: Fifty years ago, the terms ecology, environment, habitat, biome, and global warming were unheard of. Now, the environmental movement, led by such organizations as the National Audubon Society, the Nature Conservancy, the National Wildlife Federation, and the Sierra Club, is fighting to make a difference.

Bibliography

Abbott, F. 1906. *Birds and Flowers about Concord, N.H.* Concord, New Hampshire: Rumford Printing.

Adler, B., Jr. 1996. *Outwitting Squirrels.* 2d ed. Chicago: Chicago Review Press.

Allen, R. P. 1947. *The Flame Birds.* New York: Dodd, Mead and Co.

American Bird Conservancy. 1997. *All the Birds of North America.* New York: Harper Collins.

American Ornithologists' Union. 1998. *Check-list of North American Birds.* 7th ed. Washington, D.C.: American Ornithologists' Union.

Audubon, J. J. 1967. *The Birds of America.* 7 vols. New York: Dover.

Austin, O. J. 1961. *Birds of the World.* New York: Golden Press.

Bagg, A., and S. Eliot. 1937. *Birds of the Connecticut Valley in Massachusetts.* Northampton, Massachusetts: Hampshire Bookshop.

Ball, A. E. 1936. *American Land Birds.* New York: Tudor.

Banks, R. C., J. Barlow, and M. Crench. 1973. Bird collections in the U.S. and Canada. *Auk* 90 (1): 136–190.

Bateman, R. 1985. *The World of Robert Bateman.* New York: Random House.

Bellrose, F. C. 1980. *Ducks, Geese and Swans of North America.* 3rd ed. Harrisburg, Pennsylvania: Stackpole Books.

Bent, A. C. 1919–1968. *Life Histories of North American Birds.* 26 vols. Washington, D.C.: U.S. Government Printing Office.

Bent, A. C., and W. Zimmerman. 1992. *Life Histories of North American Woodpeckers.* Bloomington: Indiana University Press.

Bernstein, C. 1996. Netting a dream at Dolly Sods. *Birding Magazine* 28 (5): 436–439.

Bird Observer. 1994. *A Birder's Guide to Eastern Massachusetts.* Colorado Springs, Colorado: American Birding Association.

Bird Watcher's Digest. 1996. A tribute to Roger Tory Peterson. *Bird Watcher's Digest* 19 (12): 16–33.

Bolles, F. 1893. *At the North of Bearcamp Water.* Boston: Houghton Mifflin.

Brandt, H. 1951. *Arizona and Its Bird Life.* Cleveland: Bird Research Foundation.

Brynildson, I., and W. Hagge. 1990. *Birds in Art.* New York: Konecky and Konecky.

Burleigh, T. D. 1959. *Georgia Birds*. Norman: University of Oklahoma Press.

Cahalane, V. 1947. *Mammals of North America*. New York: Macmillan.

Cantwell, R. 1961. *Alexander Wilson*. New York: J. B. Lippincott.

Carlson, K. 1974. *Birds of Western North America*. New York: Macmillan.

Carson, R. 1962. *Silent Spring*. Boston: Houghton Mifflin.

Chapman, F. M. 1901. *Bird-Life*. New York: D. Appleton.

Chapman, F. M. 1907. *The Warblers of North America*. New York: D. Appleton.

Chapman, F. M. 1966. *Handbook of Birds of Eastern North America*. New York: Dover.

Choate, E. 1985. *The Dictionary of American Bird Names*. Cambridge, Massachusetts: Harvard Common Press.

Connor, J. 1988. *The Complete Birder*. Boston: Houghton Mifflin.

Cruickshank, H. 1968. *A Paradise of Birds*. New York: Dodd, Mead.

Curson, J., D. Quinn, and D. Beadle. 1994. *Warblers of the Americas: An Identification Guide*. Boston: Houghton Mifflin.

Dawson, W. L. 1923. *Birds of California*. San Diego, California: South Moulton.

Dearborn, N. 1903. *The Birds of Durham and Vicinity*. Master's thesis, New Hampshire College of Agriculture and Mechanic Arts.

de Kiriline, L. 1954. The voluble singer in the tree-tops. *Audubon* 56: 109–111.

Delorey, A. 1996. *A Birder's Guide to New Hampshire*. Colorado Springs, Colorado: American Birding Association.

Deming, L. 1999. White Mountain National Forest breeding bird surveys. *New Hampshire Audubon Magazine* 35 (6).

Devlin, J., and G. Naismith. 1977. *The World of Roger Tory Peterson*. New York: Times Books.

Dunn, J., and K. Garrett. 1997. *Warblers*. Boston: Houghton Mifflin.

Dunne, P. 1999. *The Feathered Quest*. Boston: Houghton Mifflin.

Eaton, E. H. 1910. *Birds of New York*. Vol. 1. Albany: University of the State of New York.

Eaton, E. H. 1914. *Birds of New York*. Vol. 2. Albany: University of the State of New York.

Ede, B. 1991. *The Art of Basil Ede: Wild Birds of America*. New York: Harry N. Abrams.

Ehrlich, P. R., D. S. Dobkin, and D. Wheye. 1988. *The Birders Handbook*. New York: Simon and Schuster.

Evans, H. E. 1993. *Pioneer Naturalists*. New York: Henry Holt.

Forbush, E. H. 1925–1929. *Birds of Massachusetts and Other New England States*. 3 vols. Boston: Commonwealth of Massachusetts.

Fraker, R., and K. Carlson. 1997. A closer look: spectacled eider. *Birding Magazine* 29 (6): 491–495.

Friedman, J. 1971. Further information on the host relations of parasitic cowbirds. *Auk* 88 (1): 239–255.

Gabrielson, I. N., and F. C. Lincoln. 1959. *Birds of Alaska*. Harrisburg, Pennsylvania: Stackpole.

Gerrone, G. S. 1999. Don't blame it on the cowbird. *Bird Watcher's Digest* 21 (5): 61.

Gibbons, F., and D. Strom. 1988. *Neighbors to the Birds.* New York: W. W. Norton.

Godfrey, W. E. 1986. *The Birds of Canada.* Ottawa: National Museum of Canada.

Greenewalt, C. 1960. *Hummingbirds.* New York: Doubleday.

Griscom, L., and A. Sprunt Jr. 1957. *The Warblers of North America.* New York: Devin-Adair.

Halle, L. J., Jr. 1947. *Spring in Washington.* New York: William Sloane.

Halpren, D., and D. Frank, eds. 1996. *The Nature Reader.* Hopewell, New Jersey: Ecco Press.

Hammond, N. 1986. *Twentieth-Century Wildlife Artists.* Woodstock, New York: Overlook Press.

Harrison, G. H. 1976. *Roger Tory Peterson's Dozen Birding Hot Spots.* New York: Simon and Schuster.

Harrison, H. H. 1975. *A Field Guide to Birds' Nests.* Boston: Houghton Mifflin.

Harrison, H. H. 1984. *Wood Warblers World.* New York: Simon and Schuster.

Howell, A. H. 1924. *Birds of Alabama.* Montgomery: Department of Game and Fish of Alabama.

Ingraham, S. 1998. Spotting scopes. *Birding Magazine* 30 (1): 70–74.

Jacques, F. L. 1957. *Outdoor Life's Gallery of North American Game.* New York: Outdoor Life.

Jacques, F. P. 1973. *Francis Lee Jacques: Artist of the Wilderness.* Garden City, New York: Doubleday.

Kalell, H. W., and D. S. Maehr. 1990. *Florida's Birds.* Sarasota, Florida: Pineapple Press.

Kastner, J. 1986. *A World of Watchers.* San Francisco: Sierra Club Books.

Kaufmann, K. 1997. *Kingbird Highway.* Boston: Houghton Mifflin.

Keenan, P. E. 1998. *Wild Orchids Across North America: A Botanical Travelogue.* Portland, Oregon: Timber Press.

Kilham, L. 1992. *Woodpeckers of Eastern North America.* New York: Dover.

Lansdowne, J. F. 1966. *Birds of the Northern Forest.* Boston: Houghton Mifflin.

Lansdowne, J. F. 1968. *Birds of the Eastern Forest.* Vol. 1. Boston: Houghton Mifflin.

Lansdowne, J. F. 1970. *Birds of the Eastern Forest.* Vol. 2. Boston: Houghton Mifflin.

Leopold, A. 1987. *A Sand County Almanac.* New York: Oxford University Press.

Lincoln, F. C., and S. R. Peterson. 1979. *Migration of Birds.* Circular 16, U.S. Department of the Interior, U.S. Fish and Wildlife Service, Washington, D.C. Northern Prairie Wildlife Research Center Home Page. http://www.npwrc. usgs.gov/resource/othrdata/migratio/migratio.htm (Version 16JAN98).

Lowery, G. H., Jr. 1955. *Louisiana Birds.* Baton Rouge: Louisiana State University Press.

MacKenzie, J. P. S. 1977. *Birds in Peril.* Boston: Houghton Mifflin.

Marcham, F. 1971. *Louis Agassiz Fuertes and the Singular Beauty of Birds*. New York: Harper and Row.

May, J. B. 1935. *The Hawks of North America*. New York: National Association of Audubon Societies.

McBurney, H. 1997. *Mark Catesby's Natural History of America*. London: Merrell Holberton.

McCaddin, J., ed. 1988. *Duck Stamps and Prints: The Complete Federal and State Editions*. New York: Hugh Lauter Levin Associates.

McClure, H. E. 1944. Nest survival over winter. *Auk* 61 (3): 384.

Mearns, B., and R. Mearns. 1992. *Audubon to Xantus*. New York: Harcourt Brace Jovanovich.

Meinzer, W. 1993. *The Roadrunner*. Lubbock: Texas Tech University Press.

Merriam, C. H. 1894. Laws of temperature control on the geographical distribution of terrestrial animals and plants. *National Geographic Magazine* 6: 229–238.

Mlodinow, S. G., and M. O'Brien. 1996. *America's 100 Most Wanted Birds*. Helena, Montana: Falcon Press.

Morris, A. 1998. *The Art of Bird Photography: A Guide to Professional Techniques*. New York: Amphoto.

Morse, D. H. 1989. *American Warblers*. Cambridge, Massachusetts: Harvard University Press.

National Audubon Society. 1998. The century of conservation. *Audubon Magazine* 100 (6).

National Geographic Society. 1960. *Wild Animals of North America*. Washington, D.C.: National Geographic Society.

National Geographic Society. 1965. *Water, Prey, and Game Birds of North America*. 2 vols. Washington, D.C.: National Geographic Society.

National Geographic Society. 1999. *A Field Guide to the Birds of North America*. 3rd ed. Washington, D.C.: National Geographic Society.

Northern Prairie Wildlife Research Center. 1998. Home page. Available via http://www.npwrc.usgs.gov/resource/othrdata/migratio/migratio.htm

Oberholser, H. 1974. *The Bird Life of Texas*. 2 vols. Austin: University of Texas Press.

Ohr, T. 1999. *Florida's Fabulous Natural Places*. Tampa, Florida: World Publications.

Palmer, R. S. 1949. *Maine Birds*. Cambridge, Massachusetts: Harvard College.

Pearson, T. G., ed. 1917. *Birds of America*. New York: Garden State Publishing.

Peattie, D. C. 1939. *A Gathering of Birds*. New York: Dodd, Mead.

Peters, H. S., and T. D. Burleigh. 1951. *Birds of Newfoundland*. Boston: Houghton Mifflin.

Peterson, R. T. 1948. *Birds over America*. New York: Dodd, Mead.

Peterson, R. T. 1957. *The Bird Watcher's Anthology*. New York: Bonanza Books.

Peterson, R. T. 1980. *A Field Guide to the Birds*. 4th ed. Boston: Houghton Mifflin.

Peterson, R. T., and J. Fisher. 1955. *Wild America*. Boston: Houghton Mifflin.

Peterson, R. T., and R. Hoglund. 1994. *Roger Tory Peterson: The Art and Photography of the World's Foremost Birder*. New York: Rizzoli.

Peterson, R. T., and V. M. Peterson. 1993. *Baby Elephant Folio of Audubon's Birds of America*. New York: Artabras.

Pettingill, O. L., Jr., ed. 1965. *The Bird Watcher's America*. New York: McGraw-Hill.

Phillips, A., J. Marshall, and G. Monson. 1964. *The Birds of Arizona*. Tucson: University of Arizona Press.

Pierson, E., J. E. Pierson, and P. Vickery. 1996. *A Birder's Guide to Maine*. Camden, Maine: Down East Books.

Pranty, B. 1996. *A Birder's Guide to Florida*. Colorado Springs, Colorado: American Birding Association.

Reed, C. 1914. *The Bird Book*. Garden City, New York: Doubleday, Page, and Co.

Ridgely, B. 1988. *Birds of the Squam Lakes Region*. 2d ed. Holderness, New Hampshire: Squam Lakes Association.

Riley, L., and W. Riley. 1992. *Guide to the National Wildlife Refuges*. New York: Macmillan.

Ripley, S. D. 1977. *Rails of the World: A Monograph of the Family Rallidae*. Toronto: M. F. Feheley.

Savage, C. 1995. *Bird Brains*. San Francisco: Sierra Club Books.

Schorre, B. 1998. *The Wood Warblers*. Austin: University of Texas Press.

Sibley, D. 2000. *The Sibley Guide to Birds: Field Identification*. New York: Alfred A. Knopf.

Singer, A. 1983. *Birds of North America*. New York: Golden Press.

Skutch, A. 1973. *The Life of the Hummingbird*. New York: Crown.

Smithsonian Migratory Bird Center. 1991. *Birds over Troubled Forest*. Washington, D.C.: Smithsonian Migratory Bird Center.

Sprunt, A., Jr. 1954. *Florida Bird Life*. New York: Coward-McCann.

Sprunt, A., Jr., and E. B. Chamberlain. 1949. *South Carolina Bird Life*. Columbia: University of South Carolina Press.

Stokes, D., and L. Stokes. 1996a. *Stokes Field Guide to Birds* (*Eastern Region*). Boston: Little, Brown.

Stokes, D., and L. Stokes. 1996b. *Stokes Field Guide to Birds* (*Western Region*). Boston: Little, Brown.

Stout, G., ed. 1967. *The Shorebirds of North America*. New York: Viking.

Stratton-Porter, G. 1910. *Music of the Wild*. New York: Doubleday, Page.

Sutton, G. M. 1980. *Bird Student: An Autobiography*. Austin: University of Texas Press.

Sykes, P., Jr. 1997. A closer look: Kirkland's warbler. *Birding Magazine* 29 (3): 220–227.

Taylor, R. 1995. *A Birder's Guide to Southeastern Arizona*. Colorado Springs, Colorado: American Birding Association.

Teale, E. 1951. *North with the Spring*. New York: Dodd, Mead.

Terborgh, J. 1989. *Where Have All the Birds Gone?* Princeton, New Jersey: Princeton University Press.

Terres, J. K. 1980. *The Audubon Society Encyclopedia of North American Birds*. New York: Alfred A. Knopf.

Terres, J. K. 1991. *Things Precious and Wild*. Golden, Colorado: Fulcrum Publishing.

Thornton, V., and B. Thornton. 1999. *Chasing Warblers*. Austin: University of Texas Press.

Torrey, B., and F. Allen. 1962. *The Journal of Henry D. Thoreau*. Vol. 5. New York: Dover.

Tucson Audubon Society. 1995. *Finding Birds in Southeast Arizona*. Tucson, Arizona: Tucson Audubon Society.

Tveten, J. L. 1993. *The Birds of Texas*. Fredericksburg, Texas: Shearer.

Veit, R. R., and W. R. Petersen. 1993. *Birds of Massachusetts*. Lincoln, Massachusetts: Massachusetts Audubon Society.

Wadsworth, B.-M. 1964. To a roadrunner. *Arizona Highways* 40 (8).

Weidensaul, S. 1989. *Duck Stamps: Art in the Service of Conservation*. New York: Gallery Books.

Weidensaul, S. 1999. *Living on the Wind*. New York: North Point Press.

Wild, P. 1986. *Pioneer Conservationists of Eastern America*. Missoula, Montana: Mountain Press.

Williams, T. 1996. Seeking refuge (America's wildlife refuges). *Audubon Magazine* 98 (3): 34–53.

Williams, W. 1989a. *Birds of the Northeast*. Tampa, Florida: World Publications.

Williams, W. 1989b. *Water Birds of the Northeast*. Tampa, Florida: World Publications.

Wilson, A. 1808–1814. *American Ornithology*. New York: J. B. Lippincott.

Wright, M. O. 1897. *Birdcraft*. New York: Macmillan.

Zickefoose, J. 1999. Ivory-billed woodpecker. *Bird Watcher's Digest* 21 (5): 28–43.

Zimmer, K. 1985. *The Western Birdwatcher*. Englewood Cliffs, New Jersey: Prentice-Hall.

Index of Bird Names

Boldface numbers indicate pages with photos.

anhinga, 106, 119
auk, 196
  great, 135, 243
avocet, American, 127

baldpate, 119
bittern, American, 114
blackbird, 189, 197
  red-winged, 37, 98, 119
  rusty, 185
bluebird, 32, 51, 85, 197
  eastern, 190, 202
bobolink, 32, 179, 189–190, 197, 199
brant, 129
bunting, snow, 215, 226

canvasback, 60, 149, 150
caracara
  Audubon's. *See* caracara, crested
  crested, 119
cardinal, 51, 65, 197
  northern, 29, 70, 90, 178
catbird, 23, 37, 178
  gray, 197
chat, yellow-breasted, 48, 49, 197

chickadee, 21, 30, 31, 32, 33, 197, 202, 219
  black-capped, **29**, 30, 32, 199, 227
  Mexican, 80
condor, California, 219
coot, 106, 150
  American, 119
cormorant, 150
  double-crested, 119, 174
cowbird, 53, 188
  brown-headed, 60, 197–198
crane, sandhill, 119
creeper, brown, 51
crossbill, 21
  white-winged, 215
crow, 32, 42, 51, 52, 53, 119, 201
  fish, 119, 128
curlew, Eskimo, 243

dickcissel, 128
dove, 243
  ground-, 119
  mourning, **22**, 90, 119, 201, 243
  rock, 17, 28
  white-winged, 70, 90
dowitcher, 119
duck, 51, 60, 145–156, 196, 202
  American black, 51, 60, 124

duck (continued)
    harlequin, 88, 149, **151**, 153–154
    Labrador, 243
    mottled, 119
    paddle, 128
    ring-necked, 119
    ruddy, 60, **124**, 150
    tree. *See* whistling-duck
    wood, 21, 32, 60, 98, 124, 149,
        150, 221

eagle, bald, 30, 119, 196, 200, 201
egret, 51, 124, 128, 152
    American, 114, 119
    cattle, 103, 119
    great, **125**
    reddish, 119, 128
    snowy, 103, 114, 119
eider, 150
    common, 151, **152**, **153**
    king, 152
    spectacled, 152
    Steller's, 152

falcon, peregrine, 126, 201
finch
    house, 23, 65, 178, 230
    purple, **23**, 135, 230
flamingo, greater, 119
flicker, 128, 166
    northern, 23, 166–167
    yellow-shafted, 23, **225**
flycatcher
    fork-tailed, 50
    least, 37
    olive-sided, 177
    scissor-tailed, 101, **102**, 223, 227
    vermilion, 89, 218
    yellow-bellied, 142
frigatebird, magnificent, 119

gadwall, 60, 119, 124
gallinule, 119, 150
    purple, 106, 114
gannet, northern, 123, 130–136,
        131, **132**, 135
goldeneye, common, 32, 146
goldfinch, 21, 32
    lesser, 65, 70
goose, 150
    blue. *See* goose, snow
    Canada, 60, 122, 149
    Ross's, 148
    snow, 60, **123**, 124
goshawk, northern, 201
grackle, 53, 119
    boat-tailed, 119
    great-tailed, 98
grebe, 150
    pied-billed, 119
grosbeak, 21
    black-headed, 70, **71**
    blue, 65, 70, 176
    evening, 135
    pine, **26**, 142
    rose-breasted, 23, 178, 215, 223
ground-dove. *See* dove, ground-
grouse, 196
    ruffed, **197**
    spruce, 185
guillemot, black, 130, 133–135, **134**
gull, 130, 196
    Bonaparte's, 119
    great black-backed, 53, 142, **143**
    herring, 30, 53, 119, 142
    laughing, 128
    ring-billed, 110, 130

harrier, northern, 119, 128
hawk, 30, 31, 32, 88, 128, 196, 201,
        216

Cooper's, 31, 90, 128, 167
gray, 89
marsh. *See* harrier, northern
red-shouldered, 118, 119
red-tailed, **2**, 119, 128
sharp-shinned, 30, 128
hawk owl, northern, 233
hen, heath, 243
heron, 124, 128, 196, 202
great blue, 30, 119, 201
green, **113**
little blue, 106, 114, 119
tricolored, 106, 119
hummingbird, 65, 82–93, **96**, 196
Allen's, 84, 85
Anna's, 89
black-chinned, 84, **85**, 89, 96, 98
blue-throated, 83, 89
broad-billed, 84, 89
broad-tailed, *96*, **97**
calliope, 83, *96*
cinnamon, 89
giant, 85
magnificent, 83, 89
rivoli. *See* hummingbird, magnificent
ruby-throated, 83, 84, 85, *96*, 167
rufous, **84**, 85, 89, *96*
violet-crowned, 84, 89

ibis
glossy, 114, 119, 128, 152
white, **106**, 119

jay, 42
Arizona. *See* jay, Mexican
blue, **13**, 21, 32, 53, 119, 128, 215
Mexican, *68*, 168
Steller's, 157
junco, 51, 200, 219

kestrel, American, 32, 119, 128
killdeer, 119, **195**
kingbird, 50
eastern, 119
tropical, 89
western, 65, **66**, 70, 218
kingfisher, 201
belted, 119, *196*
kinglet
golden-crowned, 51
ruby-crowned, 43, *68*
kite
Mississippi, 103, 105, 116
swallow-tailed, 116, **117**, 119, 227
kittiwake, black-legged, 130
knot, red, 124

lark, horned, 140, 226
limpkin, 119, **120**
loon, 150, 174
common, 142, 191

magpie, 42
black-billed, 221
mallard, 60, **149**
martin, purple, 119
meadowlark, 32, 119, 189, 190, 197, 199
eastern, 179, 188–189
western, 188
merganser, 32, 150, 227
common, 146, 147, 149
hooded, 145, **146**, 147, 149, 221
red-breasted, 147, 222
mockingbird, northern, 23, 29, 51, 119, 178, 179, 186, **187**
murre, 196
common, 130

nighthawk, common, 191, 196

night-heron
  black-crowned, 233
  yellow-crowned, 106, **107**
nutcracker, Clark's, 42, 169
nuthatch, 21, 32
  brown-headed, 111
  pygmy, 80

oldsquaw, 155–156
oriole, 197
  Baltimore, 23, 192, **193**, 201, 215
  hooded, 65, 70
osprey, 128, 201
ovenbird, 43, 46, 76, **198**, 199, 202
owl, 32, 68, 76, 201
  burrowing, 119
  great gray, 233
  great horned, 31, 201
  short-eared, 51
  snowy, 51, 233
oystercatcher, 192

parakeet, Carolina, 243
parula, 35, 39, 43, **44**, 53
pelican, brown, 119
petrel. *See* storm-petrel
pewee. *See* wood-pewee
phainopepla, 65
phalarope, 171–172
pheasant, 196
phoebe, 37, 70, 119
  black, 89
pigeon, 241
  common. *See* dove, rock
  passenger, **242**, 243
  sea. *See* guillemot
pintail, 119, 124, 149
pipit, American, 140
plover, 28
  black-bellied, 124

piping, 53, 192
poorwill, 82
puffin, Atlantic, 130
pyrrhuloxia, 90

quail, 88
  Gambel's, 65, 70, 98, **218**
  harlequin. *See* quail, Montezuma
  Mearn's. *See* quail, Montezuma
  Montezuma, 86, **87**, 88

rail, clapper, 219
razorbill, 130
redhead, 60
redpoll, 21
redstart, 35, 39, **41**, 42, 43, 53, 128,
    223, 226, 227
  American, 79
  Kaup's, 79
  painted, 68, 72, 76–79, **77**, **78**,
    221
roadrunner, 94–100, **95**, **99**, 227,
    232
robin, 26, 28, 30, 31, 37, 51, 119,
    142, 167, 192, 230
  American, 21, **25**, 197, 201, 227

sandpiper, 126
  least, 119
  spotted, 37
sapsucker
  red-breasted, 168
  yellow-bellied, 167
scaup, lesser, 119
scoter, 155
  black, 155
  surf, 155
  white-winged, 155
scrub-jay, 111
seagull, 132

shoveler, northern, 60, 119, 127
shrike, 30, 188
  loggerhead, 119
siskin, 21
  pine, 135, 142
skimmer, black, 119, 175, 222
sparrow, 45
  Bachman's, 111
  black-throated, 90, 91
  desert. *See* sparrow, black-
    throated
  English. *See* sparrow, house
  field, 37
  fox, 142, 179
  house, 28, 65, 90, 190
  savannah, 119, 140, 142
  song, 37, 104, 142, 179, 188, 196,
    197
  swamp, 142
  white-crowned, 43, 215
  white-throated, 23, 51, 142, 179
spoonbill, roseate, 104, 119, **120**,
    121, 227, **228**, 233
starling, European, 21, 27, 28, 53,
    179, 190
stilt, black-necked, 110
storm-petrel
  Leach's, 172
  Wilson's, 172, **174**, 175
swallow, 32, 98
  bank, 37
  barn, 37, 196, 215
  cliff, **196**
  tree, 37, 119, 127, 128, 192
swan, 150
swift, 82
  chimney, 196
  white-throated, 68

tanager, scarlet, 23, **37**, 223

teal
  blue-winged, 60, 119, 124, 126,
    127, 214, 215, 226, 227, 232
  green-winged, 60, 119, 124, 126,
    149
tern, 28, 53, 201
  Caspian, 119
  common, 215
  Forster's, 119, 128
  royal, 119
thrasher, 230
  brown, 179
  curve-billed, 90
thrush, 23, 37, 179, 227
  Bicknell's, 182–185
  gray-cheeked, **180**, 182–184
  hermit, 23, 51, 179–183, **180**, **181**
  Swainson's, 179, **180**, 182, 183
  wood, 23, 179–185, **180**
titmouse, bridled, 89
towhee, 119, 230
  canyon, 65, 70
trogon, 223
  elegant, **67**, 68
turnstone, 124

veery, 179, **180**, 183, **184**, 185, **195**
vireo, **199**
  blue-headed, 43
  Hutton's, 68
  Philadelphia, 185
  red-eyed, 23, 188
vulture
  black, 119
  turkey, 119, 128

warbler, 34–53, 72, 128, 142, 176,
    199, 203, 218, 219, **220**, 224,
    230–232
  Bachman's, 46, 52, 221, 243

warbler (continued)
  bay-breasted, 35, 37, 46, 53, 222
  black-and-white, 35, 39, **41**, 43,
    76, 223
  blackburnian, 35, 37, 46, 53, **220**
  blackpoll, **36**, 37, 43, 46, 53,
    137–138, **139**, 140, 222
  black-throated blue, 39, 42, 43,
    46, 48, 49, 53, 128
  black-throated gray, 68, 70
  black-throated green, 39, **40**, 43,
    46, **47**, 53, 188
  blue-winged, 52
  Brewster's, 52
  Canada, 35, 52
  Cape May, 37, 46, 49, 52, **220**
  cerulean, 53, 56, **57**
  chestnut-sided, 37, 39, 43, 177
  golden-cheeked, 46
  golden swamp, 55–61, 162
  golden-winged, 52, **220**
  Grace's, 80
  hooded, 56, **57**, 176
  Kentucky, 53, **175**
  Kirtland's, 52, 188
  Lawrence's, 52
  Lucy's, 59, 76
  MacGillivray's, 89
  magnolia, 35, 39, 43, 52, **220**,
    222
  Nashville, 72
  orange-crowned, 49, 52, 137
  palm, 53, 119, 128
  pine, 45, 53, 111
  prothonotary, 49, 58, **59**, 76, 105,
    162, 222, 227
  red-faced, 72, 76, **77**, 79, **80**, 221,
    222
  Swainson's, 52
  Tennessee, 37, 46

  Wilson's, 35, 43, 52, 89, 137, **138**,
    139, 142
  worm-eating, 52, 56
  yellow, 35, 39, 72, 89, 137, 142,
    197, 198
  yellow-rumped, 43, 45, 46, 48, 49,
    50, 53, 128, 129, 137–138, 140,
    141
  yellow-throated, 37, 39, 43, 49,
    50, 53, 56, 72, 128, 176
waterthrush, northern, 37, 42, 137,
  142
waxwing, 167
  bohemian, 23, **24**
  cedar, 23, **24**
whip-poor-will, 190–191
whistling-duck, 32, 150
  black-bellied, 105
widgeon, 60, 124
  American, 128
  Eurasian, 128
willet, 228
woodpecker, 32, 158, 177, 196, 197,
  201
  acorn, 68, **69**, 70, 168, 223
  Arctic three-toed. *See* wood-
    pecker, three-toed
  black-backed, 169–170, 185, **217**
  downy, 30, 32, 158, **159**, 164–165
  golden-fronted, 107
  hairy, 32, 158, 165
  ivory-billed, 108, 116, 161, 219,
    221, 222, 223, 234–236, **235**,
    239–243
  ladder-backed, 162. *See also*
    woodpecker, three-toed
  Lewis's, 168–169, 218
  pileated, 159–162, **160**, 218, 223,
    227, **237**, **238**, 239–240,
    241–243

red-bellied, 21, 106, 162, **163**, **164**, 168

red-cockaded, 111, 168

red-crested. *See* woodpecker, pileated

red-headed, 21, 168, 223

three-toed, 169–170, 185, 218

white-headed, 157–159, **158**

wood-pewee, 188

western, 70

wren, 60, 202

Bewick's, 89

cactus, **90**, 91

Carolina, 128

house, 192, **194**

rock, 179

winter, 177, 186

yellowlegs

greater, 119

lesser, 119

POSTSCRIPT

After the success of *Wild Orchids Across North America* in 1998 and the first discussions with Timber Press about this volume, I began plans for *Wild Plants Across North America*. Unfortunately, I have been diagnosed with ALS, commonly known as Lou Gehrig's Disease—and the third volume in the trilogy will have to wait. My new plan is to take this opportunity to thank my readers for their many letters of appreciation, the reviewers who have been so kind in their praise, and Neal Maillet of Timber Press, whose idea it was in the very beginning to take a chance with me.

Thanks one more time and peace everyone!

PHILIP KEENAN, spring 2001

Publisher's note: A week prior to his death on 30 August 2001, Philip was able to look over a set of proofs of this book.